Spiritual Blueprint

How We Live, Work, Love, Play, and Pray

James L. Papandrea, MDiv, PhD

Liguori
LIGUORI, MISSOURI

Imprimi Potest:
Thomas D. Picton, C.Ss.R.
Provincial, Denver Province
The Redemptorists

Published by Liguori Publications
Liguori, Missouri
To order, call 800-325-9521
www.liguori.org

Library of Congress Cataloging-in-Publication Data

Papandrea, James Leonard.
    Spiritual blueprint : how we live, work, love, play, and pray / James L. Papandrea.—1st ed.
        p. cm.
    ISBN 978-0-7648-1892-9
    1. Christian life—Catholic authors. I. Title.
    BX2350.3P34 2010
    248.4—dc22

                                                                                    2009044788

The author gives special thanks to Steve Miller for all the inspiration and advice over the years and for permission to quote from "Fly Like an Eagle."

Liguori Publications, a nonprofit corporation, is an apostolate of the Redemptorists. To learn more about the Redemptorists, visit Redemptorists.com.

Printed in the United States of America
14 13 12 11 10 5 4 3 2 1
First edition

For my parents, James and Nancy Papandrea, mediators of God's unconditional love and support in my life. Thank you for giving me the increasingly
rare gift of a functional home in which to grow up. Somehow you taught
me I could be anything I wanted to be, without letting me do everything
I wanted to do!

Let your father and your mother be glad;
let her who bore you rejoice.
Proverbs 23:25

Contents

Introduction

The **Five Homes** and the Image of God

THE PROBLEM

We live in a world that's over-stimulated and over-stressed. That may seem like an obvious statement, but it needs to be clarified. It is not meant to be a criticism of contemporary society, modern technology, or progress. It is not a melancholy wish for the "good old days" before things got so crazy. Contemporary society, technology, and progress provide us with opportunities that our parents and grandparents didn't have. Some of them are very important, such as developments in medicine and communication. Others are just for enjoyment, such as the ability to carry thousands of songs around with you and listen to them at any time. All these things are good and worthwhile. Therefore the problem is not technology or progress, and the solution to the problem is not found in ridding our lives of modern conveniences or comforts. It *is* possible to live a life of peace and fulfillment within the contemporary world.

On the other hand, there are things in our lives that cause us stress and rob us of peace. Some of these things come at us from our environment, and some are caused by choices we make and things we do. This book is designed to help you clarify what aspects of your life cause you stress and rob you of peace, hope, and happiness. Then you will be guided in how to make some changes in your life so that you can live with less stress, more peace of mind, and look forward to a more hopeful future. Of course, change means having to let go of the way things are, and sometimes the unknown can be scary. But don't worry; the journey you will take with this book will allow you to choose what you want to work on first, and you will be able to start with those changes that are the most comfortable.

So if the problem is not technology or the media (although I have my issues with the media), and if it's not the ever-quickening pace of contemporary culture, what is it? Although these things can contribute to the problem, the actual problem is a lack of order that prevents us from seeing and enjoying the good things in life. In other words, when we experience a lack of peace, hope, and fulfillment in life, it is often because we are overwhelmed by the anxiety that comes from feeling that life is chaotic and out of control. Maybe you don't think "chaos" is the best way to describe your life, but even if only a few things are out of whack, those things can overshadow the rest of life and prevent you from counting (and enjoying) your blessings. Whenever this happens to any of us, we are tempted to see the glass as half empty—or worse, it feels like the glass is completely empty.

THE SOLUTION

The solution to the problem, then, is to turn chaos into order. In fact, this is what God does when God creates. In Genesis, the first book of the Bible, we are told: "The earth was a formless void and darkness covered the face of the deep, while a wind from God swept over the face of the waters" (Genesis 1:2). All that existed was chaos, and chaos was all that existed. Then God created order by separating the day from the night and the land from the waters. In a way, this is how you will create order out of chaos in your life, by dividing your life into five areas that you can work on one at a time, and the result will be less anxiety and more peace. When we achieve some measure of order in our lives, we can take stock and evaluate what is good and what needs work. Then we can work on the things that need our attention without feeling overwhelmed.

There is a lot of debate over how to interpret the creation accounts in Genesis. One thing is certain, however. No matter how you interpret the details of the creation story, one of the most important lessons to be learned from the beginning chapters of Genesis is that we are created in the image of God (see Genesis 1:26–27). But what does it mean to be created in God's image? Certainly it doesn't mean a visible or physical image, since God is pure Spirit. But then what *does* it mean? I believe there are five aspects to our humanity that reflect the image of God. As humans, we are: creative, active, rational, loving, and spiritual. Each of these aspects is roughly related to one of five areas of life, or what I call the "five homes." Every person needs to attend to each one of these five areas of life. In other words, every person needs to build for himself or herself five homes: a home for your hands (where you work); a home for your body (where you live); a home for your mind (where you play); a home for your heart (where you find love); and a home for your spirit (where you pray). As you go through the pages of this book, you will learn what each of these means to you. But first, let's look at how each of us is made in the image of our Creator.

WE ARE CREATIVE

God is creative, and as humans made in the image of God, we are also creative. Of course we cannot create *ex nihilo*, or "out of nothing," as God can, but God has given us the ability to create in a way that is like God himself. We can even create life, when two of us get together and a baby is born. But what makes humans truly unique in the world is our capacity to create and appreciate things designed for their aesthetic value. This includes art but is not limited to it. It can also include crafts, architecture, even elegantly written computer code. I would also say that the act of cleaning something or someplace is an act of creating order out of chaos. The point is that humans create. Birds can make sounds and beavers can make dams, but only humans can write a song or paint a mural or carve a sculpture or build a monument.

Since we are creative as God is creative, we are born with a deep-seated need to find ways to express our creativity. Often, part of the anxiety of our lives comes from a feeling of unfulfilled (or unexpressed) creativity. We will explore the concept of creativity as we look at two of the five homes. The first one will be the home for your hands—your work. But since it is often not possible that a person's job can completely fulfill his or her need for a creative outlet, we will also explore creativity in the context of the home for your mind.

It should be mentioned that each human is created unique so that there are no two of us the same. God has intentionally made you as a one-of-a-kind masterpiece. You are unique, and you are priceless. That also means there are no two relationships with God that are the same. I will have more to say about this later, but for now it is important to allow yourself the freedom to live a life that does not have to look like anyone else's. God does not expect you to conform to anyone else, either in your external life or in your internal prayer life. You are made in the image of God, who is infinite creativity. Therefore, God has given you the great gift of your own individuality.

WE ARE ACTIVE

God didn't just create the world and then sit back and let it run on its own steam. God continues to sustain the universe and even intervene in human history throughout time. Therefore, God is eternally active. As Christians, we believe that the most important intervention of God in human history was the coming of Jesus Christ. He is the divine Word of God who became human (John 1:14). This "becoming human" we call the *Incarnation*. The Incarnation took place to reconcile humanity to God and establish a new relationship between God and humanity. In order to do that, to interact with humans, Christ had to take on a body as part of his full humanity.

Therefore, in addition to being active, God is relational. In other words, God is not some impersonal force, God is personal and wants to have a relationship with the humans he created in his own image. Similarly, we were created to be active and relational. In fact, we were created so that we are not complete without personal relationships. Of course one of the big differences between us and God is that God is pure Spirit, and therefore God can be active through his will alone, and God can be relational through his Spirit. And yet in Jesus, the Divine took on humanity, including a body, in order to interact with us. As humans, we are active and relational through our bodies. Therefore, this aspect of our creation in the image of God is primarily related to the home for your body. However, since we were created to be in relationship with others, it also relates to the home for your heart and the home for your spirit. We'll look at this in detail later, but for now it is important to keep in mind that the human body is a good thing. It is not evil, dirty, or anti-spiritual. We were created to have bodies and to be physical beings, and all that God created is good (see Genesis 1:31). Our bodies are an essential part of what makes us who we are, because it is our bodies that allow us to act and interact.

WE ARE RATIONAL

God is rational, and therefore we are rational. We do not operate merely on instinct, driven only by the desires of bodily functions and the compulsion to eat and procreate. On the contrary, we are intellectual beings created with free will and with the ability to make conscious decisions. Of course, that means we are also held responsible for our decisions and for the consequences of those decisions. We are self-aware, in the sense that we have the ability to analyze and evaluate

ourselves and to live intentionally, rather than just letting life happen to us. However, many people live with anxiety and even depression because they feel like they lack the ability to live intentionally. They believe they are powerless and are therefore trapped in a world that drags them through time, offering little choice and little hope—like a hamster on a wheel. This book will help you and encourage you to live intentionally, living life by choice rather than letting life just go by as if it's something that happens to you. Our rationality is a gift from God, and therefore God expects us to be thoughtful, intentional, and to exercise free will. This aspect of our creation in the image of God is primarily related to the home for your mind, but it affects every area of life in one way or another.

WE ARE LOVING

The apostle John said: "God is love, and those who abide in love abide in God, and God abides in them" (1 John 4:16). There are many passages in Scripture that speak about love (see 1 Corinthians 13). They all agree that the ultimate source of love is God, and also that we as humans have a responsibility to reflect the love of God to others. As people created in the image of God, we have a capacity for love that goes way beyond instinct, protection of family members, or even loyalty. We have the ability to love unselfishly, and even to have a compassion that would motivate us to make personal sacrifices for the sake of strangers. Unfortunately we don't always live up to our potential, but the potential is there nevertheless. In fact, we have more than the potential; we have the perfect example and teacher in Jesus Christ, who was so motivated by compassion for people that he risked his reputation and eventually gave his life to offer reconciliation with God. As you might guess, this aspect of our creation in the image of God is primarily related to the home for your heart. However, this is not only about romantic relationships. It is about living as a person in relation to others, as opposed to living in isolation. Many people live with feelings of sadness and depression because they feel isolated and alone. There are ways out of loneliness, and we will look at some of them. Part of the answer to isolation is becoming part of a community, which also relates to the home for your spirit.

WE ARE SPIRITUAL

God is pure Spirit, and we are created to be spiritual beings, with the capacity for an ongoing relationship with our Creator. In fact, we were created for the very purpose of relationship with God. This relationship is normally expressed in three ways: corporate worship (loving God by going to church), personal devotion (loving God through private prayer), and social responsibility (loving God by loving your neighbor). Needless

to say, this aspect of our creation in the image of God is related primarily to the home for your spirit. And since we are created for a relationship with God, no human person can truly be fulfilled in life without a relationship with God and with other people who are also in relationship with God. Many people who think they have their lives in order nevertheless live with a nagging uneasiness because they have neglected this part of life. They may reject religion as a crutch or a naive delusion, or simply as something they don't feel they need, but nevertheless they live with an emptiness that only God can fill. On the other hand, we have to keep in mind that the solution is not a passive adherence to a cookie-cutter religion or an unthinking conformity to someone else's version of spirituality. This is because each of us is unique, and each one of us was created to have our own unique relationship with God that is personal and intentional.

WHY FIVE?

Maybe is it a coincidence that there are five aspects to our creation in the image of God (as I have outlined them) and five areas of life that I call the five homes. Maybe not. In the world of the Bible, numbers had symbolic significance, and the number five seems to have been used in the ancient world as a symbol for the human person. We have five senses; we have five fingers and toes on each hand and foot. There are five extremities on our body (two legs, two arms, and the head). You get the idea. The point is that there are five aspects of our humanity that come from our creation in God's image, and these are roughly related to the five areas of life, all of which need to be fulfilled for a person to be truly happy. In order to have a healthy and balanced life, none of the five homes can be ignored, because if we lack any of the homes, that part of life will feel "homeless" and we will live with an uneasiness that can cause anxiety, sadness, and depression. So your five homes are…

A HOME FOR YOUR HANDS

This is your job, your work. The home for your hands is not really the place where you work, as in the building or office itself, but it is the world within which you work. Your occupation, your field, and to a certain extent, also the team of colleagues with whom you work. All of this goes together to make your job into something that can be life-giving or life-draining. Since you are created in the image of God who is creative, you are also creative, and the home for your hands is one place where you fulfill your need to be creative. Remember that when I say you have a need to be creative, I don't mean that it has to have something to do with art. Being creative simply means producing something that contributes to the world around you and enhances your own life or the life of your family.

Your job is one main way you participate in society, by contributing something to it.

A HOME FOR YOUR BODY

This is your actual home, where you live. Whether it is a house, an apartment, or your parents' basement, it doesn't matter. The point is that your home, like your job, can be a place that reduces stress or a place that increases stress. It *should* be the place where your body rests and is rejuvenated, and since you are active in the world and relate to other people through your body, if your body's home is not doing its job, then every other aspect of your life could suffer.

A HOME FOR YOUR MIND

The home for your mind includes many things you do that are not part of your job. It could be hobbies, sports, watching movies, or anything you do for recreation. This is the world of play, but it is vitally important for your health and happiness. All work and no play doesn't just make Jack a dull boy, it kills him—slowly at first, but then all too suddenly. One extremely important role that the home for your mind plays is in giving you additional creative outlets when your job doesn't provide enough creativity. A home for your mind gives you an opportunity to use parts of your brain that might not otherwise get used. It also gives you the ability to exercise parts of your personality that might otherwise be left dormant. God created you rational and creative, and this area of life is where you express yourself.

Speaking of exercise, believe it or not this is where you will start to think about getting in shape, if you're not already. You might think that physical exercise would belong to the home for your body, but actually it doesn't—it belongs to the home for your mind, for several reasons which we will explore later. For now, just think of it this way: your house may be the home for your body, but your body is the home for your brain! There is a deep connection between mind and body, and consequently between self-image and physical fitness. However, you can rest assured that since no two of us are created alike, we will not be comparing your body image to any other people as if there is a standard or ideal. We won't be talking much about diets, pounds, or calories. We will only be talking about feeling good about ourselves and being healthy enough to do the things we want to do for as long as possible.

A HOME FOR YOUR HEART

Your heart's home is found in relationships. This includes a significant other or romantic relationship, but it is not limited to that. It also includes friends, family, and community. We will explore how to enhance each of these, and there will be specific suggestions for those who are single and those who are married. Since God is love, and God is relational, God has created us with the capacity for real love and the need for real companionship. The giving and receiving of love and acceptance is essential for a healthy and happy life.

A HOME FOR YOUR SPIRIT

Finally, the home for your spirit is your relationship with God as expressed through your church community and religious tradition. This may be the one that gets ignored or short-changed the most. It is ironic that we all seem to have a subconscious desire to be our own highest authority; however, we can't really handle the responsibility, so trying to be our own higher power only leads to more stress. What we really need is to belong to something bigger than ourselves where we are not the highest authority and where we can submit to a power greater than ourselves. That power should be our Creator, and the something bigger than ourselves is the faith community to which we belong. In this way, we will also find some of the love and acceptance that we need from our fellow believers.

Ultimately, as Christians we are all members of the universal Church, the body of Christ, and therefore we are part of the communion of saints, that great "cloud of witnesses" made up of all Christians of all places and all times (see Hebrews 12:1). So we do belong to something much greater than ourselves, and "the gates of Hades will not prevail against it" (Matthew 16:18).

ORGANIZATION, NOT COMPARTMENTALIZATION

The purpose of this book is to help you create order in your life by segmenting life into the five areas that we are calling the five homes. This segmentation is meant to allow you to work on one area at a time so that you don't feel overwhelmed by trying to deal with the whole thing at once. But it should be said that we are only segmenting life for the sake of organization and order. We are not compartmentalizing different parts of our lives as if they exist separately, nor are we implying that one area of life doesn't affect the others. I have already noted how the distinction of mind and body is a bit artificial. This is even more true with the distinction of mind and spirit, and in fact, the apostles who wrote the New Testament would probably have assumed that mind and spirit were one and the same. So we have to be careful not to act as though we can separate these areas of life in actual practice. For example, our spiritual lives cannot be something that we attend to on Sundays only. And we certainly cannot follow the example of those who have believed that what we do with our bodies does not affect our spirits (see 1 Corinthians 6:19–20). All five of these areas of life are interrelated. This means that when any of them are not right, one can drag the others down. But it also means that as you begin to work on each area, the work you do

in one area will make each of the others easier to deal with.

I encourage you to read the whole book before you begin to work on any particular area(s). After a discussion of each of the five homes, there will be a reflection section that will help you think through and evaluate the status of each home. Each reflection section will help you decide whether that particular home needs to be rebuilt, remodeled, or just redecorated. Or maybe everything's going pretty well with some of your homes, and those homes can be appreciated. At the end of the book will be another reflection that will help you summarize all you've discovered, and finally you will be guided through the process of creating an action plan. At that time, you will have the opportunity to decide which of the homes to work on first, and you will create a plan for following through until you have built each one of your five homes and brought them all into order.

You will be able to begin immediately after you finish reading this book and doing the reflections. However, it may take some time to get through all five homes, so don't rush the process. You are on a journey, and every day will bring new ways to look at life, as well as make improvements to your life. Try to keep in mind that life is a journey, not a destination. Therefore, I hope you will resist the temptation to focus on the end of the process as a goal. In other words, resist the temptation to say to yourself, "I can't wait until I'm done with this." The truth is you may never be done, since you may find that when you've worked on all five of your homes, you can go back and start with the first one again and make even more improvements in your life. Live the process—*enjoy* the process—because you are starting on a new and exciting chapter in your life, and rushing it will not make it go faster; it will only dilute the results. Be patient, and live each day intentionally. Trying to rush through to get to an end will only shortchange the process of living intentionally. Jesus said: "So do not worry about tomorrow, for tomorrow will bring worries of its own. Today's trouble is enough for today" (Matthew 6:34). We have to take things one day at a time.

We began by stating the problem. Too many people live with too much stress. They go through each day with a feeling of anxiety that comes from a life with too much chaos and too little order. This daily chaos leads to feelings of helplessness and hopelessness. Too often people think of the future with a sense of dread, or at least a sense of fatalism, that their lives are out of their control and that another day means another round of the hamster wheel. They feel like a rat in a maze—as though they're in a rat race, and even if they should win the race, they would still be a rat. The solution to the problem is to bring peace and hope into your life. Peace comes through order and through relationships. Hope is a positive outlook on the future, which comes from gratitude for what you have and from feeling like you have some control over your life. You can increase the peace and hope in your life, and this book will show you how. You can also be assured that God wants to give you the gifts of peace and hope. The promise of Jeremiah can apply to you. God says: "For surely I know the plans I have for you...plans for your welfare and not for harm, to give you a future with hope" (Jeremiah 29:11).

1

What Are You? Identity, Vocation, and Occupation

WHAT WOULD YOU SAY if someone walked up to you on the street and asked, "What are you?" Most people would probably not give it much thought and simply respond by talking about their job. "I'm an electrician," or "an accountant," or "a project manager," or whatever. But what if the question was asked at a time when you were between jobs? Then it gets harder to answer. If I'm not working right now, what am I? Or what if you don't have a traditional job outside the home? If my work is raising children and managing a household, does that count? The question becomes more than just about what you do for a living; it becomes a question of identity.

You've probably had the experience of having to fill out a form that included a box for occupation. Did you ever feel like that little one inch box wasn't big enough to do justice to your life's work? In fact, for more and more people, a life's work cannot be summed up in one or two words. It's becoming quite rare to spend one's entire career in the same field, let alone the same job. I would argue that the very definition of *career* is changing. If you think of a career as a consistent job or series of upward moves in a single field, then very few people have only one career in life anymore. I prefer to think of the concept of a career as a lifetime of work that makes up our journey from education to retirement. But that journey is probably not going to take a straight path. The path will have lateral moves, unexpected turns, and even some times that feel like we're not moving at all. All of this is normal, and it is *not* a sign of failure. To be part of the workforce in the twenty-first century means that one's career will include multiple jobs and often multiple professions, with multiple changes in direction—and some of them will be changes that bring disappointment. But again, this is not failure; this is simply the reality of living in a world where you can't control every variable.

The question, "What are you?" is not the same thing as asking what you do for a living—it is a question of identity. If you answer the question with a job description, you are defining your identity by your occupation. The problem with this is that if you have to change jobs (especially against your will), you risk a crisis of identity. Or if you are simply dissatisfied with your job, you risk that your dissatisfaction will affect your self-esteem. No, you are far more than your job, and you are far more valuable than your salary or paycheck. Therefore, we should never define ourselves by what we do. Every person needs an understanding of his or her own identity that will not change, even if everything else in life should change.

In reality, there are three concepts that often get confused, but they are not the same. The three concepts are *identity*, *vocation*, and *occupation*. Let's look at them one at a time.

IDENTITY

Your identity is what you are and who you are, but it is not defined by what you do. That's because what you are and who you are does not change when what you do changes. To talk about a person's true identity, we have to go back to the reason we were created in the first place. We were created to have a relationship with God, and we were created in the image of God, so therefore our identity is defined in relation to God. As Christians, we find our relationship with God through our identification with Jesus Christ as our Lord and Savior. The apostle John wrote: "But to all who received him, who believed in his name, he gave power to become children of God" (John 1:12). By identifying with Christ, we have become children of God, and herein is our identity. If someone were to ask you, "What

are you?" the correct answer would be, "I am a Christian—I am a child of God."

Who you are is defined by *whose* you are! It is not defined by what you do. It is also not defined by your social status, since social status can also change. Popular literature and films are full of "rags to riches" as well as "riches to rags" stories. Unfortunately, even marital status can change, and therefore even this is not a good way to define yourself. If your identity is bound to your work or your standing in the community or even your role as a husband or wife (or for that matter any relationship), it can feel as though the rug is pulled out from under you if these things change. Finally, the things you acquire and own are possibly the worst things to attach to your identity. If you define yourself by your possessions, then you don't own them—they own you! And if they are lost, what then? In fact, a healthy identity rejects accumulation simply for accumulation's sake. We'll explore that thought later, but the point is that defining your identity on the basis of anything that can change or be lost is like building a house on a foundation of sand (Matthew 7:24–27). If the sand shifts, the whole house can fall down. Instead, a healthy identity is built on the only thing that cannot change or be lost.

Saint Augustine, the fifth-century bishop from North Africa, wrote that unhappiness (and sin) comes from fear. The fear is really an expression of the anxiety that comes from loving the wrong things. He said that if we love the things we own, or if we love the prestige or power that comes with position or anything else the world offers, we can never be truly happy, since we will always live with the fear of losing what we love. Or if we are obsessed with acquiring what we don't yet have (the Bible calls this *coveting* something), then we live with the fear of never having it. The only way to be truly happy—in other words, the only way to live without that fear and anxiety—is to orient our love toward the one we can never lose and who never changes: God. Even loving another person should not be our primary love, because relationships change. If we define our identity based on another person, we can lose a sense of who we are if we lose that person or if the relationship changes. But even if we don't lose that person, the *fear* of loss can erode our happiness, causing us anxiety, jealousy, and ultimately leading to sin and—ironically—broken relationships. The only way to happiness is to make God our primary love in life and to define ourselves in relation to God. Then we know our identity is built on a solid foundation, and even if everything else were to change around us, who we are will not change, because God will not change.

I once wrote a song based on this concept from Augustine. The song is called "Never Mind the Piano," and the second verse is addressed to God:

When everyone else is absent,
I can still feel you here
You're the only one that I can love
without feeling that fear
And you know my heart is restless
until it finds its rest in you
And though my body's feeling older,
my soul, it feels brand new

Because our identity is defined by our relationship to God, to a certain extent it is also defined by our relationship to each other. In other words, as children of God, we are also brothers and sisters of each other. And while we should not define ourselves by our relationships with other individuals, still there is a sense in which our identity is connected to God's collective people, the Church. As believers in Christ, we are members of Christ's body, the universal Church. By virtue of our baptism, we belong to something far greater than ourselves or our immediate circumstances. No matter what branch or denomination of the Church we attend, we really all belong to the same worldwide Church. In fact, as I have already indicated, a healthy identity requires belonging to something greater than yourself, where you are not the highest authority and where everything doesn't revolve around you. Therefore, identity and community are connected—but not just any community. I would caution against finding your identity in membership in a club, organization, or political cause, or even a particular denomination of the Church, since even your denomination can disappoint you. Only in the universal Church is it safe to define yourself, since doing so is really identifying with Christ rather than with an institution and its leaders. We will have more to say about this later when we look at the home for your spirit.

When we find our identity in our relationship with God through Christ and his Church, we are defining ourselves by the one thing that will remain stable, even if everything else in life should fall apart. This is the only safe way to define yourself, because only God is completely trustworthy as a solid foundation on which to base your self-awareness and self-image. If you can answer the question, "What are you?" with the affirmation, "I am a Christian—I am a child of God," then even an unexpected job change can be seen as adventure or as a clean slate, as opposed to a threat. Even if you have to move to a new city, this does not have to shake your foundation, because God goes with you.

VOCATION

The word "vocation" literally means "a calling." Most people actually have two vocations, a primary and a secondary. Your primary vocation is the one that involves religious vows. If you are married, that is your primary vocation. No matter how many jobs you may have throughout your lifetime, your marriage is your first calling and should always take precedence over any other vocation. If you are ordained or a member of a religious community, these vows are your primary vocation. In those denominations where clergy are also married, I would argue that the marriage takes precedence over the ministry for many reasons, not least of which is for the sake of the children. In any case, the religious vows you took, whether to a spouse, to your church, or to a religious community, constitute your primary vocation. No other calling should ever cause you to be unfaithful to those vows. We will have more to say about relationships and marriage when we discuss the home for your heart. The focus for now is on the secondary vocation.

The secondary vocation is not necessarily the same as one's occupation, though it can be. Vocation is more than a job. It is a "calling," which implies a pull from some force, drawing or driving a person toward a particular mission in life. That force may very well be God, or it may be simply the result of the talents we were born with and the way we were raised. I do believe, however, that when a calling comes from God, it is accompanied by the spiritual gifts to fulfill that calling. You will have the opportunity to explore your spiritual gifts in the first reflection, but for now, think about how a person's feeling of being "called" comes from the need to express who we are in the world. We all have an inborn need to exercise the talents and gifts we have. This is related to the need to be wanted and needed, and to be useful. We as humans have a need, not just to belong, but to *contribute.* This is intimately connected to the way community plays a part in our identity. When this need to belong and contribute to something greater than ourselves is not expressed in a healthy way, such as in the Church, a person is easily tempted to express it in unhealthy ways, such as in a cult or a gang. The point is that your secondary vocation is most likely related to your spiritual gifts and talents and to your unique personality. Therefore, the more your occupation can overlap with your secondary vocation, the more fulfilling it will be.

We also have a need to express ourselves through creativity. This doesn't necessarily mean something "artsy." Many people think they are not creative, simply because they are not interested in (or good at) creating art. But since we are all created in the image of a creative God, there is no one who is not creative in some way. It is often just a matter of trial and error until a person finds the right creative outlet for him or her. But it becomes a problem when a person's creativity is suppressed, and this can lead to an uneasy feeling— a feeling that life is being wasted—and eventually even to depression.

Finally, it is important to point out that a person's secondary vocation may change throughout life. You may be called to one thing for a certain part of your life and then called to something else later. As we grow, our relationship to the world around us changes, and so the way we contribute to the world might also change. To put it another way, God may call us to one thing, only to call us to something else later. But no experience is wasted, as everything we have done and are doing prepares us for what we will do.

OCCUPATION

Your occupation is your job. It's what pays the bills. Most people have to work hard for most of their lives. Even those who are retired have worked hard for many years to earn the right to work less later in life. Unfortunately, however, some people work too hard and end up sacrificing the enjoyment of life in the present for some future goal. There are two things everyone should know about their occupation:

You have to live while you work.

Most people will work for decades before they get to retire. Unfortunately, many people will never retire. Some will die before retirement. Others will not make enough money in their careers to live a life of complete leisure after age sixty-five or even seventy. The point is, if you wait until later to live, you will miss out on life. You must not live as though you're saving life for later. You may think that you are making sacrifices now for a better life later, but if you are living without peace and happiness right now, that sacrifice is too great. Life is a journey, not a destination, and if you wait to enjoy life, you may miss it completely. Or you may find that you are not healthy enough or strong enough to enjoy it later. The purpose of work is to pay for life. Therefore, pay for your life with your work, don't pay for your work with your life! Maybe you've heard the expression, "Work to live; don't live to work."

Your job can't save you, but it can kill you.

We probably all know someone whose health suffered from a life of overworking. Unfortunately, the health effects of "workaholism," with its attendant problems of inadequate sleep and poor eating habits, to name only two, are well-documented. But many people continue to overwork themselves, knowing the health risks, yet justifying their lifestyle as one of "providing for the future." They would tell you that they are working for the security of a well-financed retirement. But as we know, sometimes the very people who worked so hard for their future never live to enjoy it (see Luke 12:15–34). The truth is, security is not found in money. As recent economic events have proven, real security and peace of mind are not in bank accounts or investments or the stock market. Real security is found in God, and only in God. I know this sounds like one of those pious statements that's easy to say and hard to live by. It's true that

putting your trust in God for your future takes faith, but God is faithful. We can trust God because God is trustworthy. This is not to say that we can sit back and expect God to pay for our retirement. We still have to work for a living and save for the future. But the key to happiness is found in the *balance* of working for the future and living in the present. It's about not waiting to enjoy life and not postponing living until later, but still being responsible to the future.

Remember the story of Goldilocks and the Three Bears? Papa Bear and Mama Bear represent the extremes, but Goldilocks was always looking for that happy medium—the balance between the extremes. Ones of the keys to happiness is to train yourself to think like Goldilocks, looking for that balance. Whenever you're in a situation where you are tempted to go to the extreme, ask yourself, "What would Goldilocks do?" (WWGD).

The goal of building a home for your hands is to merge your secondary vocation with your occupation as much as possible. In that way, your job can be that outlet for expressing your talents, gifts, and creativity, making it as fulfilling and satisfying as possible while allowing you to enjoy your life along the way. Of course, not everyone has a job that fulfills all of these things. In that case, we will explore how hobbies and other activities can fill in the gaps when we look at building a home for your mind.

2

A **Home for Your Hands**: Where You Work

Think about your occupation. If you are retired or between jobs, think about the occupation in which you've spent the most time. Why did you choose that field? Did you intentionally go in that direction, or was it chosen for you? If you fell into it for some reason other than your own choosing, why did you stay? Because it paid the bills? Because it provided security? Because it did more than pay the bills, and it provided a certain standard of living? Or was it because you enjoyed the work?

Why *do* you stay in your current job? Why will you go back to work tomorrow or Monday? Is it simply for the paycheck? Is it because you're good at what you do, and you get some satisfaction out of doing it? Is it because what you do is necessary for society, and you are providing a service that the world cannot live without? Your answers to these questions are not right or wrong, but if you answer them honestly, they will tell you something about yourself. The real bottom line question is, "What do you hope to accomplish with your job?" Think about that for a minute.

When you answered that question, "What do you hope to accomplish with your job?", did you answer it with a long-term answer (save for retirement, accomplish a goal) or with a short-term answer (pay the bills this month, pay for college next semester, fund a vacation)? Again, neither one is wrong. However, the best answer would be a combination of long-term and short-term considerations. Here's another question to ask yourself: "How will you know if you are a success?" Maybe you can already see where this is going. Don't define success only in terms of a long-term goal. You do not have to wait until retirement or until the end of your life to be a success. You can be a success right now. That's because the purpose of your occupation is not at the end of your life, or even at retirement. The purpose of your occupation is to give you a lifestyle, and that means now. But be careful—when you read the word *lifestyle*, does it bring up images of a certain standard of living that includes a particular level of comfort and accumulation of possessions? If so, what are you willing to trade for that kind of lifestyle? Often people end up trading peace, as they live with a lot more stress so they can provide that standard of living. The question is whether the standard of living is worth the stress, or whether a life with less stress would make a better lifestyle.

Success is not a goal or a destination; it is a way of life. This is good news, because it means that there is really no such thing as failure, since there is always time to start again with a clean slate. Failure is only failure if you quit when you're down. And every time you get up again is another success story. Too many people define success and failure in terms of ultimate goals, and so they deny themselves the joy of living in the present, because they are so focused on (and anxious about) the future. They pressure themselves to work harder and harder out of fear that they might not work hard enough to make it to that goal by which they define success. But life is like the manna in the desert (see Exodus 16). You can't save it for tomorrow. You have to live it today. And so the only real risk of failure is the possibility of looking back on a life that was postponed until it was too late.

Building a home for your hands means investing yourself in an occupation that balances preparing for the future with living life now. For some people, this might mean backing away from aggressively working for future security in order to spend more time (and money) on living now. It might also mean balancing the present and the future by allowing yourself a healthier lifestyle now and settling for a simpler lifestyle in retirement. All of this requires an element of trusting God for the future, since we cannot control the future, no matter how much money we have. Of course, if you are not saving for the future at all, that can also cause anxiety. Our aim is a healthy balance of living in the present and preparing for the future. Like Goldilocks searching for the happy medium that is "just right," our goal should not be an accomplishment or the end of some process, but a lifestyle of balance along the way. Before we can get into the details of how this might work, we have to take a serious look at how we think about money and finances.

REDEFINING THE CONCEPT OF WEALTH

One of the best books I've ever read on finances is *Rich Dad, Poor Dad,* by Robert T. Kiyosaki. While not necessarily written from a Christian perspective, this book helped me to redefine what I think about wealth and financial success, not in terms of net worth, but in terms of lifestyle. In other words, wealth is not about money in the bank; it's about the kind of lifestyle that one can afford. However, the problem is that most people use their money to buy themselves a stressful lifestyle. Or worse, they buy that stressful lifestyle on credit, and then the debt makes them even more stressed. We may think that more is better, but in reality, we end up filling our lives with things that actually destroy our peace and happiness.

Our friend Saint Augustine wrote a document called *On the Trinity*, and in that document, he went off on a bit of a tangent in which he said some very interesting things. To paraphrase, Augustine basically said that you *can* have everything you want. You actually can have everything you want! If you don't have everything you want at this moment, then you have two choices. You can try to get more—but be careful—that's a bottomless pit of anxiety, because you will never be satisfied. On the other hand, you can learn to want less. You can have everything you want, if you can learn to want what you have. I know it sounds like another pious platitude, but think about what he's saying. You can be happy with less. This is good news, because less is within your reach, which means happiness is within your reach.

When we connect this idea to the other concept we got from Augustine, that if you love anything other than God you will always live with the fear of losing it, we can see that often the more we have, the more anxiety we have. More stuff means more stress. Of course, he's not saying that owning things is a sin. He's also not saying that having money or expensive possessions is a sin. But if a person spends his career working for the accumulation of money

and an abundance of possessions, then that person is robbing himself or herself of peace and happiness in the present, trading it for the possible goal of some future state that may or may not come.

LIVE WITH LESS, REDUCE YOUR STRESS

The bottom line is that it doesn't pay to chase after money. On the other hand, if you can learn to be satisfied with what you have and to want less—with fewer things comes a lower level of stress. One concrete way to put this into practice is to ask yourself this question before making any major purchase: *Will the enjoyment I get from owning this outweigh the stress it will bring into my life?* We may not realize it at the time of purchase, but often the stress of paying for, using, storing, repairing, or fueling whatever it is will actually overshadow the enjoyment of a thing. Therefore, before making a major purchase, don't think about how much you want it, or how the idea of owning it will make you feel (be careful of connecting your identity to the ownership of anything!), or what it will look like to others that you have it. Think about whether it will bring more stress into your life than it takes away. If owning it will bring more peace than stress (which assumes you can afford it without the stress of debt), then go for it! But if it will bring more stress than peace into your life, you will be happier without it.

In Jesus' parable of the rich fool (Luke 12:15–34), the rich man died with a full barn. Given the choice, there is no doubt that he would have chosen to live longer but less wealthy. If we define wealth as net worth, the man was rich. But if we define wealth in terms of a lifestyle, he was actually poor. And so is anyone who overworks themselves for the accumulation of money and possessions, and in so doing, misses out on life along the way. Life is a journey, full of changes and second chances. Don't trade happiness on the journey for a destination that may never appear on the horizon. Happiness is living a balanced life in which you can tell the difference between the things that relieve stress and the things that cause more stress, holding on to the things that make you happy and letting go of things that rob you of peace and happiness.

ARE YOU IN THE RIGHT JOB?

Now that we have disentangled your identity from your occupation and redefined wealth in a healthier way, we can begin to think about building a home for your hands. The ideal situation would be one in which your occupation matches your secondary vocation. Therefore, the first step will be to think about your secondary vocation and determine whether it is something that is or could be related to your occupation. As I mentioned above, a person's vocation is connected to his or her gifts. A list of the Gifts of the Spirit is included at the end of this book so that you can begin to think about what your gifts are. An occupation that matched your vocation would be one in which you got to use your gifts and talents as an expression of yourself and your creativity. In the reflection section in the next chapter, you will have the opportunity to think about whether your current job gives you that kind of creative outlet.

Of course, if you're reading this and thinking, *I hate my job*, then you already know you're in the wrong job. The question then becomes whether you're in the wrong field or just the wrong office. Why do you hate your job? Is it the work you have to do or the people you have to do it with? Imagine doing the same job in another situation. Would that fix the problem or not? If so, you may want to think about finding a different job in the same field. In the next chapter, you'll have a chance to think about these questions and come to some conclusions.

Whether you are evaluating your present job or looking for a new one, you have to consider where the job in question falls on what I call *the stress continuum*. There is usually a direct relationship between stress and reward in any job. The higher the stress, the higher the reward. Very low-stress jobs often don't pay as well as high-stress jobs, which makes sense, because no one would take the higher-stress jobs if they didn't pay more. The question is where you as an individual fall on the stress continuum. How much stress can you handle and still have it be worth the reward? For example, I could probably learn to be an air traffic controller and make more money than I do as a professor. However, the stress of that job would negatively affect the quality of my life. But some people thrive on that kind of stress. In fact, they would call it excitement, not stress. Thank God for them— when I fly, I want one of those people watching the screens. But far too many people work in jobs that are at a stress level that is beyond what they can tolerate and still be happy. The problem is, once in that job, people get used to living at a certain financial level, and they literally trap themselves in a job that is too stressful. They think they could not live on the lower salary that would come with a lower-stress job. They think they couldn't be happy making less money, when in reality they would be much happier!

Another example of this would be the difference between a salaried position and one based on commission. In a sales job, often the pay is entirely a percentage of sales made. These jobs usually pay well, but there is no guarantee, so that in a bad year a person could make a lot less than the previous year. Some people thrive on the challenge and do not mind the possibility of a fluctuating income. Others would find the apparent instability to be unnerving. Only you can determine what level of stress is worth the reward. However, if a job is so stressful that it affects your happiness, even when you're not at work, then it's not worth the money. There is nothing wrong with choosing a job that will pay you less but allow you to be happier, healthier, and live longer.

I know what you're thinking now. *If I take a job that pays less, and I live longer, I will outlive my savings in retirement.* It is true that if you take a job that pays less to have a healthier and happier life now, you may have to work longer, into your late sixties or even into your seventies. That's the trade-off. But you will be working a lower stress job that is more fulfilling, so theoretically you won't be so anxious to retire. The alternative is to burn yourself out, hoping to make it to retirement, and there is still no guarantee you will have enough money saved to retire earlier. You will have to decide what is right for you: how hard to work now without sacrificing all your peace and happiness on the journey; how early you can retire without ruining your health so you can't enjoy retirement; and what kind of lifestyle you expect to live in retirement as compared to your present lifestyle. Just try to think like Goldilocks—find the balance of the happy medium—and do it intentionally by deciding on a course of action rather than just letting life go by on a default setting.

SAFETY ON THE JOB

Just as the level of stress has to be worth the reward, the level of responsibility should be worth the risk. In other words, a job should be safe to take responsibility, safe to take personal risks, and even safe to make mistakes. If you have to fear losing your job every time you make a decision, that may be too much stress. The point is that while we can't expect that a job will always be *fun*, it is reasonable to expect that a person might get satisfaction from his or her job most of the time. Everyone deserves to have a job that doesn't drain the life out of them. If your job is so stressful that it drains you rather than energizes you, or if it affects your ability to enjoy life outside of the workday, it might be time to think about a change.

It would be impossible to explore every employment option within the pages of this book, but we can condense the search into a question: *Does the job drain you or energize you?* Different jobs affect different people in different ways, because we all have different personalities. Often a personality evaluation such as the Myers-Briggs inventory will prove helpful in finding the kind of work that is right for a person. But chances are, if the job energizes you, then it is close to your secondary vocation, and it is serving as a viable outlet for your gifts and creativity. If the job drains you, if you have a hard time dragging yourself out of bed to get there in the morning, or if you dread going back every

Monday, then the job may not be right for you. If this is the case, you may have to ask yourself some tough questions. Am I willing to take less pay or get more education for a job that is more conducive to my happiness? Am I willing to make other changes necessary, including possibly moving, in order to work in a job that energizes me and allows me to be happy?

Of course it may not be possible to make a job change right away (whatever you do, don't quit your job until you have another one to go to!), but the point is to make a plan so that you can be ready when the time is right, and you can think of the future with hopefulness. Eventually, though, changes will have to be made, if in fact your job is robbing you of peace and happiness. If you don't make some changes, then your job will eventually rob you of your health and possibly your life. Remember that since your identity is not in what you do, you can see change as an adventure. Anything is possible; it's just that some sacrifices may have to be made in order to realize positive change. Don't say, "I can't...." Instead say, "How can I...?" and be ready to make a plan. Don't be afraid of where change may take you. You are a child of God, and God will go with you wherever you go.

Realistically, it also may not be possible to find a job that connects with your secondary vocation as much as you would like. In that case, the goal is to get as close as possible and then consider how hobbies and other activities can fill the gap and become a creative outlet of personal expression. But this will have to wait for the chapter on a home for your mind.

One more thing is important to mention before we move on to the reflection and begin to make a plan. Remember that if you are married, your marriage is your primary vocation, and neither your secondary vocation nor your occupation should interfere with that primary calling. Therefore, your spouse has to be part of any decision that leads to major changes in your life, especially if it means a move and/or a change in standard of living. It's possible that the prospect of change will sound threatening to your spouse. It might be helpful for the two of you to work through this book together. At least keep your spouse informed about your thoughts as you go through the book, and reassure him or her that you will not make any life-changing decisions without discussing them first. It could be that when you get to the end of this book, you will choose to start with the smaller changes anyway. Either way, you can both rest assured that you will not be required to make any changes, or even any decisions, until you have finished the book and evaluated each of the five areas of life. Then it will be up to you which changes to make first.

In the next chapter (and in each reflection chapter), use the spaces in the pages to write out your thoughts on each of the questions. Write as much as you can, because you will be coming back to these reflections after you finish the book, and you will need to remember what you were thinking.

3

Reflection on the **Home for Your Hands**

SUCCESS IS A LIFESTYLE

What do you hope to accomplish with your job? _____

_____

Short term goals? _____

Long term goals? _____

Describe the lifestyle you hope to live in retirement: _____

Describe the lifestyle you would like to be living now: _____

How is the lifestyle you are actually living now different from the one you would like to live now?

_____

_____

How could you make your lifestyle now more like the one you hope for in retirement?

_____

_____

In what ways could you simplify your retirement lifestyle to enhance your present lifestyle?

_____

_____

On the other hand, are you saving enough for retirement?_____

Would you have to simplify your present lifestyle so that you can maintain

your lifestyle in retirement? _____

_____

To summarize, how could your present lifestyle and your retirement lifestyle meet in the middle?

_____

MAJOR POSSESSIONS INVENTORY

Walk around your home with a yellow legal pad. Write down every major thing you own. Include the house itself, and don't forget the car(s) in the garage!

In the margin, give each of your major possessions a rating of plus or minus. Give it a plus if owning it brings more enjoyment and peace of mind than stress. Give it a minus if owning it brings you more stress than peace or enjoyment. Take into account whether you are in debt because of this item. In other words, would you have more spending money without the loan?

Stop and thank God for all the things that have a plus in the margin. Now on a separate page, list all of the things that have a minus rating.

What would happen if you got rid of the things that cause more stress? _____

_____

What would happen if you traded in one or more of your cars for a more modest model?

_____

What would life be like without each one of the things that cause you stress? _____

_____

Which one(s) are you willing to live without, if you could have more peace and freedom? _____

_____

What steps would it take to get rid of these things?_____

_____

ARE YOU IN THE RIGHT JOB?

Do you hate your job? _____

Do you struggle with your colleagues and/or coworkers? _____

Does your job energize you or drain you? Why?_____

Does your job negatively affect your life outside of work? _____

Is it safe to take risks and make mistakes in your job, or do you worry about decisions you make?

_____

Does your job give more stress than satisfaction, or more satisfaction than stress? _____

What aspects of your job would you like to change? _____

What aspects of your job would you like to keep? _____

Would getting a different job mean changing your standard of living? _____

What would that look like? Smaller house? Different cars? Different city/neighborhood?_____

_____

THE IMPORTANT THINGS IN LIFE

What do you think about the idea that living with less means living with less stress? _____

_____

Is your house bigger than you need? _____

Do you have debt that's causing you stress?_____

_____

What could you live without that would both reduce your debt and simplify your life? _____

_____

What would people think about you if you drove a more modest car?_____

_____

What would people think about you if you changed jobs to one that paid less? _____

_____

SPIRITUAL GIFTS

*Look at the list of **Gifts of the Spirit** at the end of this book. Which ones do you have?*
Circle all that sound like you.

What do you think your calling (secondary vocation) is? _____

_____

Which of the spiritual gifts are you using at your job? Put a check by these.

How close is your current job to your calling (secondary vocation)? _____

_____

Make a separate list of those gifts that you have and that you do not use on the job.

Is your job satisfying as an expression of your personality and your creativity? _____

Do you feel like you contribute something valuable through your job? _____

_____

Is there something you have done in life (whether or not for pay) that was most rewarding? _____

_____

Would it be possible to do that for a living? _____

Is there something you did for someone else out of which you got more fulfillment? _____

_____

Would it be possible to do that for a living? _____

What kind of work would allow you to use as many of your gifts as possible? _____

_____

Are you satisfied with your occupation, or are you in the wrong field?_____

What kind of job should you be doing? _____

Would this job require more education? _____

What steps would you have to take to change jobs to get closer to your secondary vocation? _____

_____

If you are in the right job, are you in the wrong office or on the wrong team? _____

BEING GOLDILOCKS

Are you living too much in the present, too much for the future, or in balance? _____

Are you living too much for short-term goals, too much for long-term goals, or in balance? _____

Does your standard of living require a job with too much stress? _____

Would redefining "success" as a lifestyle allow you to live with more peace?_____

Evaluation

Which do you think applies to you? Circle all the statements that sound like your situation right now. Then choose one of the categories below.

Rebuild: You're in the wrong job and need to be in a different field altogether. You need to be doing something different, or maybe you're between jobs right now and need to find the right job for you. You need to determine your calling (secondary vocation) by discovering your spiritual gifts and talents. Then you need to look for an occupation that is closer to your calling.

Remodel: You're in the right field but in the wrong company or organization. You need a new job doing roughly the same thing but in a different place. In addition, there may be some significant lifestyle changes that a new job would provide. You could use the fresh start that a new job would give you. Write down any possible changes regarding your finances and major possessions. You are not making a commitment to actually make any of these changes; you are only writing them down for consideration later when you've finished exploring all five homes.

Redecorate: You're in the right job, in the right place, at least for now. You are satisfied with your current job, and your work is creative or productive enough that any remaining need for a creative outlet can be met through hobbies or other activities (the home for your mind).

However, there are some lifestyle changes you can make that would reduce your stress. Write down any possible changes regarding your finances and major possessions. You are not making a commitment to actually make any of these changes; you are only writing them down for consideration later, when you've finished exploring all five homes. Also, make a list of all of your spiritual gifts and talents that are not currently being used in your job. You will need this list to build the home for your mind.

Appreciate: You have a good home for your hands. Neither your job nor your finances are a source of stress in your life. You can be thankful for this area of life. Still, no job is perfect. Write down any of your spiritual gifts or parts of your personality that you feel remain unexpressed in your job. These will help you think about building a home for your mind. Finally, say a prayer of thanksgiving to God for your job and for the home for your hands. If you are retired and no longer need to work, thank God for your career and for the way that God provided for you and your family throughout your career.

4

The Bat Cave and the Dollhouse

ONE OF MY BEST FRIENDS is a cockapoo named Coco Bean. My wife and I live in his house. At least he thinks it's his house, but that's a good thing. I want to make it very clear that I did not pick his name. I wanted to name him Chuck Norris, but this was just one of life's little negotiations that I didn't win. When we brought Coco Bean home, we crate-trained him, which means he spent the nights in his crate. The amazing thing is that he waited until we took him out in the morning to do his business. Apparently, puppies are born with an instinct that prevents them from going to the bathroom in their own space. As time went on, his concept of his own space was expanded to include the whole house, and while there were a few accidents in the beginning, now he never goes to the bathroom in the house. But he still thinks of his crate as his own little den, and sometimes he goes in there on his own when he wants to take a nap or just be alone with his thoughts.

We can learn something from puppies. Too often we humans take our living space for granted. We disrespect it, or we fill it with clutter, or we just ignore it. But then it's not really there for us when we need it—at least not in the way we need it to be. Just as a sword has its sheath, every person needs a place to go when the battle is done for the day—a place where you know you don't have to fight for a while, where you can rest. Therefore your living space, your home, is the home for your body. This may seem obvious; however, many people still take it for granted. Maybe they feel as though the body is somehow the opposite of spirituality or rationality, and so it doesn't seem very spiritual, or very intellectual, to focus on the physical. But have you ever tried to take an exam when you had a toothache? Or hold a meaningful conversation while walking with a rock in your shoe? If your body is not happy, the rest of you can't be happy either.

It is true that we were created as spiritual beings, but we were never meant to be disembodied spirits. That idea comes from pagan philosophy. Many of the Greek philosophers assumed that when a person died, his or her spirit was simply reincarnated into a new body, and the old body was discarded. There was also a trend within philosophy (it comes from Plato) which said that the things of the spiritual realm are more real than the things of the physical realm. When these two ideas were taken to the extreme, the result was a *dualism* that led to the belief that everything from the spiritual realm was good, and everything from the physical realm was evil—including the human body. So death was seen as an escape from the "prison" of the body. Interestingly, this belief led to two very different options in practice. Some reasoned that since the spiritual world was so far above and beyond the physical world, what one did with one's body could not affect the spirit. These *libertines* concluded that it was acceptable to indulge every physical desire, as though they could wallow in the lusts of the flesh and still remain spiritually aloof. On the other hand, some reasoned that since the body was evil, it should be punished and its desires suppressed. These *ascetics* led a life of self-denial to the extreme. While it is true that some Christians have historically chosen a life of asceticism, in general, the Judeo-Christian tradition affirmed a middle way. This middle way rejects the extreme punishment of the body, because the human body is part of God's good creation. But it also rejected the irresponsibility of a "freedom" that was really hedonism in disguise.

As always, the goal is balance. We should not indulge our bodies, but we should respect them as gifts from God. Remember that it is only through our bodies that we are able to

be both active and relational. And in order to offer us a relationship with God, Jesus took on a body as an essential part of his true humanity. Therefore, our goal is not to be freed from the body as though it were a prison or some sort of curse. Our body is part of our humanity, just as it is eternally part of Christ's humanity. When we die, it is not as though we become bodiless spirits. Rather, we look forward to a resurrection body, which may be changed, but nevertheless is somehow consistent with the bodies we have now (1 Corinthians 15). The details of this are of course a mystery, but I like to think it is analogous to the difference between a caterpillar and a butterfly. If you tried to explain what a butterfly is to a caterpillar, the caterpillar would not be able to understand it. And yet it is not a different individual after the chrysalis. Therefore it would be wrong for the caterpillar to disregard his body as something to be discarded. In the same way, our bodies are an essential part of who we are, and so we take care of them, because taking care of our bodies contributes to health and happiness. In fact, the apostle Paul described the body as a home for God's Holy Spirit (1 Corinthians 6:19–20).

When I say that your body is part of who you are, I don't mean that we should see the shape of our bodies as part of our identity. Remember, the outward appearance of your body can change, and it's not good to attach your identity to anything that can change. We'll talk about physical fitness in the chapter on a home for your mind, but for now the point is that this body of yours is the only body you will ever get, and it is part of your very humanity. Therefore, when you think about building a home for your body, that home has to be a place that contributes to the health and comfort of your body, which in turn will contribute to your peace of mind and your overall happiness.

A good home for your body is one in which you can relax. It's one in which stress is relieved, not increased. It's a place where you can rest and regain energy, where you can "recharge" your mental and emotional batteries. Just like Coco Bean has his crate, your home can be the place where you go to get away from it all—like a daily vacation at the end of the work day or a weekly vacation on the weekends. Your home for your body should be like Batman's Bat Cave—your enemies can't go there. In other words, it's the place you go to get away from the daily conflicts of life and other things that cause stress. Another way of looking at it is like a dollhouse. If you have a dollhouse, you get to decide what goes in the house and what doesn't, so you are in control over the environment. That's what a good home for your body is—a place where you are in control over your environment, and there are fewer things to worry about. When you're there, you enjoy peace of mind and can rest up to be ready for new challenges that await you the next time you go out into the world.

5

A **Home for Your Body**: Where You Live

A SAFE HARBOR

Think of yourself as a ship. Every morning, you leave the port and go out to sea. The sea may be calm that day, or it may be stormy. If you work in your home, you will still face challenges that seem to toss you around like a boat on the waves. All day long you confront conflicts, make decisions, deal with difficult people, sit in traffic, and just generally manage stress. You're like that ship in the storm or the crimefighter in the city. At the end of the day, your home has to be a safe harbor where you can get away from the storm. It has to be your Bat Cave, where your enemies can't get to you. It has to be a place of peace where you can relax and recharge, because tomorrow there will be more storms and more villains to face. In other words, your home cannot be a source of stress, because if it is, you have nowhere to go to escape from the anxiety.

Too many people who suffer from anxiety and depression and who go through midlife crises or have extramarital affairs would be better off if their home was a place that relieved stress rather than created stress. The bedroom is especially important, since that's where you sleep, and a stressful bedroom can decrease both the quantity and quality of sleep that you get. Sometimes the cause of stress within the home is the relationship of the people who live there, especially if we're talking about a married couple. If you think that applies to you, be patient, and we'll talk about relationships when we look at building a home for your heart. For now it is important to admit that if you are married, part of your job as a husband or wife is to help make your home a place of peace and relaxation for your spouse. This may include listening to your spouse vent about the annoying people and other problems he or she encounters throughout the day. It may not be your first choice for dinner conversation, but chances are your spouse needs to talk about it in order to put it out of his or her mind so he or she can relax. It's up to you to help your spouse do that by being a good listener.

GET YOUR HOUSE READY FOR SALE, THEN KEEP IT

If you were to put your house on the market, your realtor would no doubt give you some suggestions for getting the house ready to be seen by potential buyers. These suggestions would probably include removing a lot of the clutter and maybe even moving or removing some of the furniture. This makes the house look bigger, more spacious, less cluttered, less busy…you see where I'm going with this? It makes the house seem *more peaceful*. So why not make it more peaceful now while you still live in it? Many people get a house ready for sale and then realize how much they like the house that way, and they wish they had made the changes long before.

Think about what your house looks like when company comes over. Now think about what it looks like most of the time. Why not treat yourself as well as you treat the company and keep the house looking great for you? Granted, you probably work harder to get the house ready for company than you want to work on a daily basis. That's true, but there are two observations I want to make. The first is that when you clean for company, you often put things away so they're out of sight. Some of these things might be things you could live without. If you don't want them around when company comes, why do you want them around for you to trip over them? Now I know that some of the things you put away are things you use regularly, but you just don't want them out when company arrives. But here's the other observation. If you put things away right after you use them, they don't pile up, creating clutter and

eyesores, and then it doesn't take so long to gather up everything that's been accumulating. In other words, if you don't want your company to see the old shoes in the middle of the living room floor, why leave them there for you to look at? Put them away, and treat yourself like company! If you don't want your company to see the dirty dishes in the sink, don't let them pile up. Wash them right away, and treat yourself like company! It sounds like more work, but it's not—the work is spread out so it's less work at any one time, and you will actually relax more when it's done. Plus, if you get rid of some of the things that clutter up your place, you will have fewer things to clean later.

LESS IS MORE

When it comes to filling up your home with your stuff, less is definitely more. A cluttered home looks busy, and busy looks stressful. By contrast, a home with more open space looks more peaceful. Therefore, one of the goals of building a home for your body is to get rid of whatever you don't need and find a place to put away the things you do need. This does not mean getting rid of keepsakes, collectibles, or heirlooms. If these things bring you enjoyment because they have sentimental value or because you like collecting them, then you should keep them. But they should have a place, a place of honor, in fact, not be just all over. If you have children, there should be a place for them to play where they can set up their toys but where you won't trip over them. Kids need their own space, too. When you go through the reflections in the next chapter, you will have an opportunity to go through everything you own and get rid of as much as possible. Does that sound drastic? Just remember, you won't be expected to get rid of anything you really want to keep. But the goal is to de-clutter your home to make it more attractive and peaceful. If you do this, you will clear away the visual white noise and leave room for the things you love to be truly appreciated. Plan to have a rummage sale or give the rest to charity.

If you are married, then of course you are not the only one who makes decisions about your living space. You will have to include your spouse in the decision to get rid of things you don't really need. In the end, you can only get rid of the things you both agree on. If there are things you can't agree to get rid of, maybe you can agree to put some away in storage (although if at all possible, I would advise against paying for storage space). For example, my wife would be perfectly happy getting rid of my old martial arts trophies. I would prefer to put them on the mantle so everyone would see them and so I could glory in my past triumphs. So they're on display in the basement. That's the compromise. You can always go back later and get those things you've put in storage or even periodically swap them out for other things. In our basement, we

also have a whole table full of knickknacks. From time to time, we'll notice something on a shelf or table that's been there so long we don't even see it any more. We take it down and put it on the table in the basement, exchange it for something that hasn't been out in a while, and then it's like we just got something new for the house.

A HOME FOR YOUR FIVE SENSES

The point of de-cluttering is to decrease the busyness of your home. When you have too much stuff around you, you are overstimulated, and it's harder to relax. This is true of all five senses, but especially the eyes. Your living space should *look* relaxing. The colors of your home should be inviting and peaceful. Lighting should be bright enough that it doesn't seem gloomy, but not so bright that it seems harsh. It is also important that the television is not on all the time. If the TV is on when no one is watching it, the flickering images seen in the corner of your eye can become agitating and stressful. Make a point to have the TV on only when you're actually watching a program.

The same goes for your ears. When the TV is on as background noise, it becomes just that—noise. And noise is stressful. If you are using the television to provide you with a sense of company, then that is a different issue. We will explore ways to overcome loneliness when we look at building a home for your heart and a home for your spirit.

In the meantime, try to resist the temptation to put the TV on from the minute you get home. Rather than the television, put on some music, preferably music that you find relieves stress. Of course, there's nothing wrong with any particular type of music. If you find that you enjoy a certain kind of music, chances are that listening to it will reduce tension. I happen to love reggae music. (It makes me happy; what can I say?) But I also recommend any style of Christian music, because listening to it will remind you of your true identity as a child of God.

When it comes to a home for your nose, we are, of course, talking about what your home smells like. Needless to say, if there are any bad smells that need to be taken care of, do whatever it takes to get rid of them. Don't allow yourself to become used to them, because you could rob yourself of the enjoyment of things that smell good in your home. It could be that your home needs more fresh air—then open some windows and air it out periodically. On the other hand, some people like scented candles. Figure out what works for you and give yourself permission to make your home smell the way you want it to. Don't forget to take your garbage out often so it doesn't make your place smell bad.

The food you serve in your home will affect both your nose and your tongue. In fact, smell is actually a big part of your sense of taste. Take the initiative to live intentionally with regard to the food you eat. Take it upon yourself to expand your taste horizons. Try new foods and new spices. Bring fruit into your home (don't forget to eat it, though, or you're just wasting money!). Think about the foods you enjoy most, and rather than only having them when you go out, learn to cook them at home.

Last but not least is the sense of touch. A good home for your body is also a good home for your skin. Pay attention to what kinds of fabrics surround you. Are you able to keep your home at a temperature that is comfortable for you? If you have to, experiment with the thermostat to find the setting that would make Goldilocks proud... "just right." I am of the opinion that it does no good to lower your heat to try to save a few pennies a year. When your furnace has to work harder to bring the temperature back up to a comfortable setting, it will undo any savings you might have realized by having the temperature lower for a while. Find the temperature you are comfortable with and give yourself permission to leave your home at that temperature all the time. Then you will be comfortable when you get out of bed in the morning and when you first get home in the evening. Of course if you are married or share your home with others, you will need to compromise on the temperature. But if you discuss it, you should be able to find a compromise that's within a few degrees of optimum. If needed, get an air conditioner, fan, or space heater for the part of the house you relax in most. The point is that no one should have to be too cold or too hot in their own home.

Speaking of temperature, it may be appropriate to ask yourself whether you are living in the right climate for you. Some people find they get a mild form of depression from a lack of sunlight. In some places the winter is just too long or too gloomy for these people to be happy. Are you the kind of person who should be living in a sunny climate year round? Or are you the type of person who needs all four seasons? It is certainly legitimate to consider moving to a different climate just because you will be happier there.

SURROUND YOURSELF WITH GOOD THINGS

Although I am a strong proponent of getting rid of as much clutter as possible, I am not advocating a minimalist existence. Remember that we are looking for balance, and empty shelves are just the other extreme from clutter. Neither extreme is desirable. You should surround yourself with the things you love. This includes things of sentimental value and things you enjoy using. If that *MAD Magazine* collection brings you enjoyment because you like looking through the old ones, then by all means, keep it. If the Hummel figurines bring you joy, then they should have a place of honor on a shelf or in a curio cabinet. But if there's a vase sitting on the shelf

that hasn't had a flower in it in twenty years, and you can't remember where you got it, then get rid of it. Old magazines you'll never read, toys and games no one plays with, pots and pans you never use, clothes you never wear—the list goes on, and they all should go. But the objective is not to live in an empty house. The objective is two things, really. The first is to create more open space for a more peaceful environment. But just as important is the second, to make room to appreciate the things that mean the most to you.

Surrounding yourself with the things you love includes living things. This can be pets or plants; even fake plants are a low maintenance option if that does the trick for you. If you have pets, you will necessarily have the things that go along with pets, such as pet food, pet toys, and maybe a litter box. Just make sure to be intentional about where these things go and make sure to have a place for the pet food and other essentials. Having a pet can bring a lot of happiness and reduce your stress, but if you're not careful, all the things that go with having a pet can also make your home feel more chaotic.

Finally, surround yourself with the things that remind you of your identity as a child of God. I've already mentioned listening to Christian music. In addition, I recommend religious art and icons, and especially crucifixes or crosses. All of these will remind you of who you are, because they will remind you *whose* you are.

Reflection on the **Home for Your Body**

YOUR HOUSE AND YOUR HOME

Are there aspects of your home that cause you stress? _____

Are your mortgage or property taxes too high for your comfort?_____

Is your house too big to clean? _____

Is your yard too big to keep up with? _____

Are you living in the right climate for your personality?_____

Do you feel "down" for a significant part of the year? _____

Taking into consideration what you answered about your home in the reflections in Chapter 3,

what would it mean for you to move from your present home? _____

_____

WOULD YOU BUY YOUR HOUSE?

What does your house look like when important company comes over? _____

What does your house look like most of the time when no company is expected? _____

What's the difference between the two? _____

What can you do to treat yourself like company? _____

_____

Take a tour of your home, going into each room, and don't forget the garage and/or shed.
In each room, write down the answers to these questions:

What is this room for? (What do we do here?)_____

Is there too much clutter in this room? _____

If the room has no specific function, what could it be if it were empty? _____

Are there any activities we would like to have room for that we presently don't? _____

Do the kids have their own space to play? _____

What would happen if we took one or more rooms and changed their purpose? _____

Walk around your home, paying attention to your senses. What does your home look like? _____

_____

What colors do you see? Do you like these colors? Are they inviting? Peaceful?_____

_____

Does your home look busy?_____

Is the lighting adequate in each room? _____

Is the TV on when no one is watching a specific show? _____

What does your home sound like? _____

Is the TV on for background noise or to make you feel connected to the world?_____

What would it be like if you had the TV off most of the time? _____

What would it be like if you had music you enjoy playing more than the TV? _____

What kind of music reduces stress for you? _____

How many CDs of this type do you own? Is it enough? _____

What does your home smell like? Are there any bad smells? _____

_____

What would you like your home to smell like? _____

_____

What does your home taste like? What kinds of foods do you like to have in your home? _____

_____

What kinds of foods might you like to add to your home?_____

What would it take to expand your food horizons? A cooking class? A new cookbook? _____

_____

What does your home feel like? Is the temperature right for you? _____

Is the furniture comfortable? _____

Is there any uncomfortable furniture? What if you got rid of it? _____

Is there some piece of furniture missing that would add to your comfort?_____

YOUR OWN BAT CAVE OR DOLLHOUSE

What is your favorite place or places to relax in your home? _____

Is there anything in those places that prevents you from relaxing? _____

Is there anything missing that would make you more able to relax?_____

Is your bedroom clean enough to be peaceful? _____

Is there anything creating a feeling of chaos in your bedroom? _____

Is there anything missing from your bedroom that would make it easier to sleep? _____

POSSESSIONS INVENTORY (CONTINUED)

Go through your entire home, including garage, basement, and shed, if you have one. Take your yellow legal pad with you, and write down everything you own. Include even the smallest things. For each item, write down two things:

WHY YOU SHOULD KEEP IT. It's OK to say, "It makes me happy," but do not use that as a default for everything! If there is no reason to keep the item, make a check mark by it.

WHERE IT BELONGS IN THE HOUSE (where it would be "put away"). If there is no place it belongs, either designate a place for it or think about getting rid of it. If you can decide to get rid of it, put a check mark by it.

What would it mean to you to get rid of all the things with a check mark?_____

_____

What steps would you have to take to get these things out of your home? _____

_____

Which things would be put into storage? _____

_____

Where will you store them? (Don't take on an extra monthly payment by getting a storage space.

If you would need to pay for outside storage space, you're not getting rid of enough!) _____

_____

What things in your home cause you stress or prevent you from relaxing? Can you get rid of these

things? _____

If not, can you store them? If not, can you move them away from your favorite relaxing spot(s)?

_____

_____

Is there a room or home office space that needs to be cleaned, with piles that need to be organized?

_____

Do you have a pet or pets that cause you stress or make your home chaotic? Does a pet need some

training that will help? _____

Do you need to organize the pet's toys, food, etc. so that they are out of the way?_____

Do you have a litterbox, and if so, where is it? Is it in the way? Does is stink? _____

Clean out your refrigerator and throw away everything old.
Do the same with the cupboards and pantry.
Organize your cupboards and closets.
Get rid of clothes you no longer wear; give them to charity or hold a rummage sale.

THE IMPORTANT THINGS IN LIFE

Make a list of the things you would want to save if the house was on fire. Why are these things

important to you?_____

_____

How are these things honored or protected in your home? _____

Would it give you peace of mind to get a fireproof box to put some of them in?_____

What do you have in your home to remind you of your true identity as a child of God? _____

Would you feel comfortable adding more of these things? If so, what? _____

BEING GOLDILOCKS

What would it look like to find the balance between the extremes of cluttered and empty? _____

What is the most comfortable temperature for you? _____

Evaluation

Which do you think applies to you? Circle all the statements that sound like your situation right now. Then choose one of the categories below.

Rebuild: You need to move. This house or home is not right for you. It is either the wrong size or it is in the wrong climate or the payments are stressful. Your current home causes more stress than it relieves.

Remodel: You're in the right home, but it needs some major changes. This could include literally remodeling, but it need not be an expense. It could mean rearranging some rooms or painting. Consider throwing a painting party, and provide pizza for all your friends who will help. Pick colors that seem peaceful to you. Consider adding some reminders of your identity as a Christian and as a child of God.

Redecorate: You're in the right home, and in general, it's in pretty good shape. But it needs to be cleaned and organized, and maybe some furniture should be rearranged. Get rid of as much as possible, de-clutter, and possibly add some reminders of your identity as a Christian and as a child of God.

Appreciate: You have a good home for your body. Neither your home nor the things in it are a source of stress in your life. You can be thankful for this area of life. If you live with someone else, write down ways that you can do more to make your home a haven of peace for your spouse or anyone else who also lives there with you. If you currently feel that your spouse is a source of stress, but everything else in the home is peaceful, allow yourself to appreciate your home for your body, and we'll deal with the relationship stress when we talk about the home for your heart. Finally, say a prayer of thanksgiving to God for your home and for the home for your body.

7

Walk the Earth: The Kung Fu Factor and the Yoga Experience

IN THE POPULAR 1970s television series, *Kung Fu*, David Carradine played Kwai Chang Caine, a Shaolin monk. He was running from the consequences of having killed a prince while defending his teacher and mentor. In a not-so-subtle allusion to the biblical Cain (Genesis 4), the hero of *Kung Fu* was forced to "walk the earth," but now acting as his brothers' keeper. He traveled throughout the old West, protecting the innocent and beating up the bad guys with his martial arts skills. This was one of my favorite shows as a kid, and as I think about it now, I believe there are two reasons why I (and so many others) found it fascinating. The first reason is the concept of the quest. Kwai Chang Caine was on a journey, and it didn't matter that he never actually reached a destination. He was on a mission, with no responsibilities other than to be a hero. I suppose it's the same reason I like King Arthur stories and James Bond films. The other reason I liked *Kung Fu* is that I was (and still am) fascinated by the concept of the fighting monk. I suppose the Christian equivalent would

be the Knights Templar, who also hold a mythical fascination for many people. Even Friar Tuck in the Robin Hood stories was known to join in on a few fights as he helped the merry band in their struggle for social justice. The fighting monk is a combination of saint and superhero. He is that paradox of a man of God who can also take matters into his own hands and defeat evil in the name of good, truth, and righteousness.

So what is it about this paradoxical mixture of contemplation and martial arts? On the surface, it should be a contradiction. The Lord says, "Vengeance is mine, I will repay" (Romans 12:19). So why do we suspend that reality in order to enjoy the stories? I suppose it is partly because humans love a happy ending where our perception of justice is upheld. We love to see good win out over evil, and we especially love to see evil characters get what's coming to them. Of course, in the television show, Caine was portrayed as a pacifist who only fought when he had to. But he always had to, and the audience was never disappointed. At the end of each episode of *Kung Fu*, Caine had saved the day, but then he just quietly moved on. "He saved others; he cannot save himself" (Matthew 27:42). Unlike Zorro or Batman, he didn't get to take off his mask and resume a life of wealth and comfort. He was doomed to continue to walk the earth, alone and marked as one who had taken a life. The very skills that made him a hero had also made him a loner. And this is part of the fascination, because he is not just a fighter, he is also a contemplative. The paradox of the fighting monk represents the paradoxical connection of the body and mind in all of us.

ON A QUEST

As humans, we can relate to Caine/Cain. We are all sinners with a less than perfect past, and we are all on a quest for redemption or, at least, for a clean slate. As I've said, life is a journey, and while we trust that there is a destination in heaven, in the present life, we have to focus on the journey one day at a time. Along the way, we look for peace, deal with conflict, and try to help others. And even though we know that our good works alone will not save us, we hope that our journey will end in the presence of God, in whom we put our trust. In the meantime, we walk the earth.

Because we are created in the image of God, we are rational and creative. This is part of what connects us to our God. Furthermore, these two concepts are intimately related to each other. In

God, rationality leads to creativity. God thought, spoke, and created. And even though we need a body to turn our will into activity, it is still true for us that thought leads to action. This can work to our advantage, or it can work against us. On the positive side, if we dream and plan something, there is little we can't accomplish. On the negative side, temptation can lead to sin if we dwell on it and give it room to settle in our minds. Of course temptation itself is not a sin, and we are not held responsible for every thought that pops into our heads, but we all know the difference between dismissing a thought and entertaining a thought. Also there are some sins that require no action. These are sins that only occur in the privacy of our own minds, sins such as lust, envy, hatred, and bigotry. The point is that in all of us, thought leads to action, and continued action becomes habit. Again this can work in your favor, as in the cultivation of healthy habits, or it can work against you—so if you're not careful with your thoughts, you can fall into unhealthy behavior—but it all begins in your mind.

When we look at building a home for your mind, we are talking about occupying your mind with healthy activity. This will do two things. It will give you an outlet of personal expression, and it will leave you less time for the unhealthy things that tempt you. We'll explore the idea of social responsibility (works of charity) when we look at building a home for your spirit. For now, just keep in mind that the more time you spend on healthy activities, the less time or energy you will have for the unhealthy ones.

THE MIND—BODY CONNECTION

By now you should see that the mind and body are connected. For me, that mind-body connection is personified in the Kung Fu factor— the fighting friar, contemplative combatant, or saintly soldier. You might prefer a less militant (and perhaps less contradictory) image, such as the Yoga experience. Yoga, sometimes combined with forms of meditation, is thought by many to be a way to clear the mind, while at the same time strengthening the body. The point is that when we talk of a home for our minds, we cannot ignore our bodies, which are a kind of mobile home for our brains. You can't make a good home for your mind without taking care of your body. As it turns out, you also can't make a good home for your spirit without taking care of and respecting your body. As we've already noted, our bodies are also a home for God's Holy Spirit (see 1 Corinthians 6:19–20).

And so we've come full circle. We began with our creation in the image of God, and it's that image of God that connects us to God, especially through our rationality and creativity. Another way to say that is that our minds connect us to God because they are created to be like God.

But our minds are also connected to our bodies, which are the instruments through which our thoughts become action. Our bodies are connected to God through the Holy Spirit who indwells us. So God connects with our mind, which connects with our body, which by our actions can draw us closer to (or farther away from) God.

Saint Augustine said something that I'll paraphrase as, "I doubt, therefore I am" (*On the Trinity*). What he meant was that sin (just like good works) begins in the mind. Doubt itself is not a sin; however, the realization that a decision has to be made is an exercise in self-awareness. True self-awareness comes from acknowledging that your identity is not in external things but in your relationship with God. To act on your self-awareness would be to distance yourself from the externals that cloud your judgment and attract you to unhealthy activity. Sin, on the other hand, comes from associating ourselves too closely with those external things. The point is not to see individual moments of resisting or giving in to temptation as ultimate successes or failures. The point is to realize that each moment and each decision is a point on the journey of life, and it is important to be moving in the right direction. If you have failures in your past, they are forgiven. The point is not where you were then, or even where you are now, but in what direction you are headed. Are you headed in the right direction?

Are you moving closer to a healthy lifestyle and closer to God, or farther away? There is no standing still; we are always either moving toward God or away from him.

In the 1991 film, *Terminator 2: Judgment Day*, the Terminator, played by Arnold Schwarzenegger, explains how the master-computer "Skynet" was able to take over the world. It became *self-aware* at 2:14 AM Eastern Time, August 29, 1997. In other words, there was a moment in time when the computer achieved the ability not just to think, but *to think about itself*, and that gave it the power to make decisions about its own future. We have probably all had experiences of self-awareness. Some of these might be called conversion experiences. Others might be called mountaintop experiences, moments of enlightenment, or even New Year's resolutions. Whatever you call it, we all need to be self-aware more consistently in life, and we all need self-assessment from time to time. Hopefully this book will help you to take stock of your present situation and make some conscious decisions about your future so that you can live intentionally from now on. Then, as you walk the earth, even when there is no destination in sight, you can have peace of mind that you're moving in the right direction.

8

A **Home for Your Mind**: Where You Play

BUILDING A HOME for your mind really means spending time doing things that make you happy. It's not too much more complicated than that. The only problem is that sometimes the things that make us happy in the long-term are not the same things that make us happy in the short-term. So we have to motivate ourselves to set aside immediate gratification in favor of some greater long-term good. In other words, sometimes we have to get off the couch and get some exercise. But if you can find the balance of short-term and long-term happiness, building a home for your mind will do two very important things for you. It will increase your confidence (self-esteem), and it will reduce stress.

Specifically, there are two kinds of activities that are part of the home for your mind. The first is the kind of activity that allows you to express yourself. We have already talked about how important it is for every person to find an outlet for his or her creativity. There is no one who is not meant to be creative, because we are all made in the image of the Creator. If you don't like to think of yourself as "artsy," here's another way to look at it. Everyone needs to be *productive*

in life, to contribute something. Even if that just means producing something that only you and your closest friends and loved ones will ever see, it still counts. We all need to express ourselves by creating, producing, or contributing something. The second kind of activity is activity that contributes to your health and long life. This, of course, would include exercise. Remember that exercise produces chemicals in your brain that actually act like a natural antidepressant. In any case, we tend to feel better about ourselves when we exercise, so again it kills two birds with one stone: we reduce stress and increase self-confidence.

ACTIVITIES THAT ALLOW YOU TO EXPRESS YOURSELF

Think about this: What kind of activity could make you forget to eat a meal? What kind of activity could so engross you that you would stay up all night and hardly notice the passing of time? We could also ask some of the same questions we considered in the chapter on a home for your hands: Is there something you did for someone else, but then you felt like you got more out of the experience than they did? What have you done that you feel was an unforgettable experience? We're talking here about your passion(s). What is it that you are passionate about? If you could make a living doing anything —your favorite thing—what would it be?

There is nothing wrong with making significant time in your life for doing the things that make you happy (provided, of course, that doing these things doesn't make someone else unhappy!). There are actually two types of activities that you can think about here. One type is active, and the other is passive. Active activities include anything from playing sports to stamp collecting. It could be artsy, like writing songs or painting; it could be crafty, like scrapbooking; or it could be something that might not seem to be creative in a traditional sense, like working on a car or training a puppy. Passive activities, on the other hand, are those that may not actually produce anything concrete, but still bring you happiness and reduce stress, such as watching movies, reading, or going out to eat. These are the things you do to relax. Just because these things are passive does not mean they don't count. It could be that they stimulate discussion and build relationships, but even if a movie only makes you laugh, that is enough. In fact, I can't emphasize enough the importance and benefit of humor and laughter. It really is the best medicine.

You will have an opportunity in the reflection section of the next chapter to write down your passions and hobbies. For now, keep in mind that what you do with your free time is not wasted time. It's very important to your physical and mental health. As I said in the chapter on the home for your hands, don't short-change your health in the present by working too much for the future. In other words, don't sacrifice all your free time now, just because you are working hard. Don't skip a vacation thinking you'll take it later. Find a way to take it sooner; you won't be sorry. If you wait, you may find that when you finally get around to it, you are no longer healthy enough to travel or some other situation prevents it.

ACTIVITIES THAT CONTRIBUTE TO HEALTH AND LONGEVITY

About a decade ago, I got on the scale and realized I was overweight. To be honest, I suspected it even before I got on the scale, which is why I put off getting on the scale for so long. In any case, the scale confirmed my suspicions. So I began a serious program of diet and exercise, and I lost forty pounds. But guess what? I found them again. And a few more on top of those. Recently, I started the whole process over again. I'm now almost to my goal weight, but how do I make sure I don't just bounce back to being overweight again? What I have discovered is that there is a very simple formula for how your lifestyle relates to your weight. It looks like this:

If your lifestyle includes:	You will:
Dieting and exercise	Lose weight
No dieting, but with exercise	Maintain your weight
No dieting and no exercise	Gain weight

Granted, this chart is very general, and I'm not that kind of doctor, but my experience bears it out. When I was not eating healthy and not exercising, I gained a bunch of weight. Big surprise, right? So I lost the weight by dieting and exercising (and it still took about two years to lose forty pounds). But then when I lost the weight, I went back to my old lifestyle of eating normally (and I was even eating more healthy) but without the exercise. So I gained all the weight back and then some. What I've realized is that even when I reach my target weight and I don't have to be "on a diet," not only do I have to continue to eat healthy, but I have to continue to exercise. If I don't, I know what will happen—I will gain weight until I'm overweight again.

We can't go into detail about dieting here, but the point is that *everyone needs exercise*. This means you. And by the way, if you didn't sweat, you didn't exercise. Of course that assumes that you are healthy enough to exercise, so make

sure you check with your doctor before starting any new diet or exercise program. If you are not healthy enough to work up a sweat, your doctor can help you with some less strenuous activities to get you started. And another thing: if you're not going to the doctor regularly, you aren't healthy. This is not a "no news is good news" situation. What you don't know *can* hurt you, so if you haven't been to the doctor in over a year, put the book down right now and call and make an appointment. I mean it.

Assuming you are healthy enough to exercise, what you do to burn calories is up to you. But it has to be something close to fun, or you won't keep up with it. If there is a sport you enjoy playing, join a league or schedule regular time to play. Sports are great because you actually accomplish both kinds of activity in one—they can be both a passion and a form of exercise. But if you're not into sports, that's OK. Find what works for you. If you need to join a gym, do it. If you are the type who prefers to exercise at home, don't be afraid to try some workout DVDs or exercise gadgets. You may have to try some things that don't work before you find the right thing, so give yourself permission to do some trial and error, even if it means you blow a few dollars on some things that don't work for you. At least you will be trying. I find that it helps to watch a TV program in which I can get absorbed, and then I almost forget I'm on the treadmill. So I buy the DVDs to avoid the commercials, and the time just flies by. For me, the fun is in watching the show, not the treadmill itself, but it still works to keep me motivated to come back to it regularly. Whatever it takes, figure out what you can do for exercise, not just to lose weight, but as an ongoing part of your lifestyle. This is not something you will do for a season or to accomplish a goal; this is something everyone needs to incorporate into their lives—for the rest of their lives.

MAKING GOOD DECISIONS

If you can incorporate significant time in your lifestyle for activities that make you happy and allow you to express yourself, as well as activities that allow you to burn off dessert, you will be healthier in both mind and body. You will have less stress and more confidence. This will give you a clearer head for making good decisions. You see, the mind—body connection is a two way street: thought leads to action, but healthy activity also leads to clear thought. We've already talked about the role of the mind in resisting temptation, but there is one thing that is worth mentioning specifically. It's something that was apparently very important to Jesus.

When Jesus taught his disciples the Lord's Prayer, he made a point to highlight the line about forgiving others by saying, "If you do not forgive others, neither will your Father forgive your trespasses" (Matthew 6:15). In other words, the refusal to forgive is itself a sin. If you hold a grudge, if you harbor anger or resentment, you are only hurting yourself. Someone once said that holding on to hatred toward another person is like drinking poison and hoping it kills that person. If you can't find a way to forgive, the anger will short circuit everything else you are trying to work on in your life.

Jesus also said we must forgive each other, "from your heart" (Matthew 18:35). Sometimes this seems impossible, since you might ask yourself, *How can I forgive when I don't feel forgiving? Wouldn't that be hypocritical if I'm not really ready to forgive?* The truth is that in the ancient world, the heart was not seen as the place where emotions or feelings come from. It was seen as the place of the will, the place where decisions come from. So in effect, Jesus was saying that we must make a decision to forgive, even when we don't feel like it. If you want to live intentionally, and if you want to improve your life, you're going to have to learn to let go of anger and resentment, or it will eventually ruin your life. As the apostle Paul said, it's normal to get angry, and anger itself is not necessarily a sin (see John 2:14–17), but "do not let the sun go down on your anger" (Ephesians 4:26–27). In other words, if you hold a grudge as if that is your right, then you have crossed the line into sin. What is more, you have allowed something into your mind that will cloud your judgment and prevent you from making good and healthy decisions.

We'll talk more about this when we look at building a home for your spirit, but for now think about this: Just as you can't consider yourself physically healthy without seeing your doctor regularly, you may also need to see a spiritual guide or mental health professional from time to time. This does not mean you've failed at anything; it just means you need help. Even a dentist cannot drill his own teeth—everyone needs help sometimes. If you can't find a way to forgive on your own, then make an appointment to see your pastor or a counselor so you can talk and pray about it and move toward letting it go.

It is hard to resist temptation in any situation, and in practice, it's impossible to resist temptation all the time. It's even harder if we try to do it on our own power. When we are able to resist temptation or when we are able to forgive, it is not by will power, but rather by surrendering the will. It is not by being strong, but by admitting we're weak that we have victory over sin. That's because the victory is not ours but Christ's, and when we are weak, he is our strength (2 Corinthians 12:10).

Even when it comes to doing God's will in life, we have to focus on the journey and not on the destination. Every day, we are faced with

opportunities to say yes to God or to say no to God. Sometimes we get it right on the first try, and we say yes. We resist temptation or we choose to forgive or we make time to do the things that are healthy. Other times we say no to God, but God always gives us another chance. As long as we are alive, the invitations from God keep coming. And the more we say yes to God, the more we build healthy habits. And all this will be easier if you have built a good home for your mind with a healthy lifestyle.

Since no two of us are created alike, God's will may be different for each of us in the big decisions of life. But in the everyday choices we face, God's will for all of us is the same. We are all expected to cultivate the *Fruit of the Spirit*, those character traits that allow us to treat each other with love, joy, peace, patience, kindness, generosity, faithfulness, gentleness, and self-control (Galatians 5:22–23). As long as you walk the earth, take life one day at a time, and focus on doing what is healthy rather than focusing on what you're not supposed to do. Then you can create good habits and learn to remove yourself from situations that give rise to temptation, rather than having to resist temptation. You will then be able to invest yourself in those things that allow you to express your true identity as a rational and creative child of God.

9

Reflection on the **Home for Your Mind**

I BECAME SELF-AWARE...

Think about one or more self-awareness moments you have had. What did you learn about yourself?

_____

_____

What decisions or resolutions did you make? _____

What promise(s) to yourself does this represent? _____

What would it look like to keep this promise?_____

What do you think about the idea that thought leads to action? _____

How has this proven true in your life? _____

_____

Can you think of a time when you thought about something but didn't act on it and now wish
you had? _____

Can you think of a time when you thought about something but didn't act on it, and now you're
glad you didn't? _____

Can you think of a time when you thought about something and acted on it and now wish
you hadn't? _____

_____

Can you think of a time when you thought about something and acted on it, and now you're glad you did? _____

What do you think of the idea that your body is home for God's Holy Spirit?_____

_____

What would it look like if you were to live each day keeping in mind that your body is home for the Holy Spirit? _____

What would it look like for you to be more self-aware on a daily basis? _____

PASSIONS AND PROJECTS

Go to the list of **Gifts of the Spirit** *at the end of this book, and compare your notes from chapter three.*

Which gifts and talents did you circle that are not fulfilled by your job?_____

Is there anything you added to the list that was not there? If so, what? _____

Is there anything that other people continually tell you you're good at? _____

Is there a cause you feel strongly enough about to get involved? _____

Is there a group of people you feel compassion for and want to help?_____

If you could spend your free time doing one thing, what would it be?_____

What kind of project could make you forget to eat? _____

What subject could keep you up talking all night long? _____

What activities make you happy? What do you look forward to doing? _____

What hobbies or sports do you enjoy? _____

Are there things you do just to relax? What are they? _____

_____

What activities would make you more relaxed and less stressed?_____

_____

How much time per week do you spend on your passions or projects? _____

_____

Is it enough? Is it too much? What would the right amount be, and how close are you to it? _____

_____

What would you have to give up to spend more time on your passions or projects? _____

_____

How can you plan to make sure to spend enough time on these every week? _____

_____

EATING HEALTHY

Think back over the last week, and write down everything you can remember eating.
Look at your calendar, if needed, to remind you where you were each day.

Would you want your doctor to see this list? (Don't have a doctor? Get one!) _____

Do you eat fast food every day? (Don't!) _____

If you're not eating healthy, is your problem quality or quantity (or both)? _____

What foods do you eat or restaurants do you go to that you later regret? _____

Make a mental note to leave these foods and/or restaurants out of your life.

EXERCISE

When was the last time you went to the doctor for a check-up? If more than a year, make an appointment! Seriously—do it. Ask your doctor about diet and exercise.

What do you like to do for exercise? (Remember, if you don't like it, you won't keep it up.) _____
_____

How often do you exercise? Do you work up a sweat?_____

What sport(s) do you like to play? _____

How often do you play? Do you work up a sweat? _____

Do you play often enough to improve your skills? _____

Are you happy with the shape you're in? _____

Are you happy with the way your clothes fit? _____

Are you holding on to clothes that don't fit? _____

Are you able to do all the things you want to do? _____

MENTAL HEALTH

Are you holding on to anger or resentment toward anyone or anything? _____
_____

Is there someone you need to forgive, if not for them, for your own health? _____
_____

Do you need to make an appointment to see your pastor or spiritual guide? _____
_____

Are there any other unhealthy habits you need to break? Smoking? Addictions? _____

_____

Do you need to look into the possibility of seeing a therapist? _____

_____

What would it be like if you saw a therapist? _____

_____

What steps would you need to take to start that process? _____

_____

BEING GOLDILOCKS

Do you spend enough time having fun? Do you spend too much time goofing off? _____

_____

_____

What is the right balance of work and play for you? _____

_____

_____

Do you spend enough time exercising? What is the right balance of rest and activity? _____

_____

_____

What is the right balance of enjoying food and eating healthy? _____

_____

_____

Evaluation

Which do you think applies to you? Circle all the statements that sound like your situation right now. Then choose one of the categories below:

Rebuild: You are inactive. You need a hobby or project to give your free time focus and purpose, and/or you are overweight and need to get in shape. Maybe you are also hiding unhealthy habits or even an addiction. Maybe you are holding on to anger or resentment.

Remodel: You are underactive. You need to step up your efforts at spending time on your passions or projects. You may need to lose a few pounds.

Redecorate: You are active but could still stand to eat healthier and/or exercise more. Or maybe you work too much and could stand to spend more time relaxing.

Appreciate: You have a good home for your mind. You participate in activities that express your personality and activities that contribute to your health. You have one or more hobbies or other activities that make you happy and that you regularly make time for. You know how and when to relax. You are not harboring anger, resentment, or bad habits. You can be thankful for this area of life. Say a prayer of thanksgiving to God for your passions or projects and for the home for your mind.

10

Heart of Glass: The Meaning of Life

IN MY OPINION, one of the best lines ever written in a song is the opening of "Heart of Glass," by Blondie: "Once I had a love and it was a gas, soon turned out/Had a heart of glass."

Classic. Like all good songwriting, this line does two things: it says something that rings true in a succinct, poetic way; and it says something the listener can identify with. Chances are good you've had your heart broken, and chances are also good that there is a song that brings that experience to mind and maybe even helps heal it.

Did you ever wonder why love songs are so popular? And did you ever wonder why breakup songs are even more popular? Part of it is because the experiences that these songs relate are virtually universal. But also it's because misery loves company, and we all know deep down that love is a risk. We just like to hear that knowledge affirmed and set to emotionally-evocative music. When you put yourself out there and offer yourself to someone else, you risk that you might be rejected. Or worse, you risk that you might be accepted for a while and then rejected when your guard is down. It could be said that love is downright dangerous. And yet we take the risk,

and we keep taking the risk, because the rewards are worth it. And when we find real love, we hope eventually to get past the risk to a place of peace and security.

God understands the risk. God continually reaches out to a humanity that rejects him (John 1:11). "God proves his love for us in that while we still were sinners Christ died for us" (Romans 5:8). In fact, we are only capable of real love because God took the initiative to show us how to love by loving us first (1 John 4:19). This is one of the ways we are made in the image of God, and in fact, this is the meaning of life—to accept God's love and to learn to love others.

THE MEANING OF LIFE

Just as your identity can only be found in your relationship with God, finding meaning in life also begins and ends with your relationship with God. The meaning of life is not in your occupation or in accomplishing goals any more than your identity is. You might be tempted to think that the meaning of life is found in having a "mission in life," some important work to do that will bring you recognition or do some good in the world or perhaps even outlive you. You might even try to find meaning in working for wealth or security. But as the saying goes, you can't take it with you. The truth is, the meaning of this life is only to be found in the one thing that you *can* take with you into the next life—relationships. The apostle Paul wrote, "And now faith, hope, and love abide, these three; and the greatest of these is love" (1 Corinthians 13:13). Have you ever wondered why love is the greatest? It's because love is the only one that is eternal. Faith will become obsolete when we see God face-to-face (see 1 Corinthians 13:13; 1 John 3:2), and hope will go by the wayside when we have the eternal life that we hope for (see Romans 8:24–25; Hebrews 11:1), but love lives on into eternity. Not only that, but the relationships we have formed with the people we love will also live on, as we are reunited with them in heaven.

Everyone wants to believe that his or her life has meaning or significance, and everyone wants to be appreciated by those around them. But your significance is not dependant on what you can *do* for the world or on what you might *produce* or *create*. Those things are great, and they are an expression of your personality, but your significance—your *value* as a person—is only dependent on having relationships with people who value you simply because they want you around. Securing for yourself a situation where you are the indispensible center of attention,

even if you could do that, would not bring you happiness and peace of mind. That's because you would have to live with the fear that it would all go away some day. Instead, peace comes from being appreciated for who you are and from feeling loved. It comes from a feeling of unconditional acceptance that amounts to a kind of security. You feel peace when you don't have to worry about being abandoned by the people you care about. This feeling of unconditional acceptance and love, when it is mutually shared among significant others and friends, is what makes life worthwhile. If you accomplish nothing in your life except creating relationships with people who will miss you when you're gone, then your life has meaning.

All this is to say that the home for your heart is in your relationships. But we're not only talking about romantic relationships. There are actually three types of relationships that you will build throughout your life. One is the romantic relationship. This usually leads to marriage with the one person whom you would call your best friend—the person you want to live with for the rest of your life. Another type of relationship is friendships. These are the people who like having you around, and you like being around them. You may not be compatible enough to live together, but you want to spend time with them on a regular basis. Some people like to have a lot of friends; others like to have a few very close friends. Either way is fine. It just depends on your personality. The third type of relationship is community. In general, this has to do with more formally-organized groups you belong to. The most important community group is, of course, your church. We'll look at this third type of relationship when we talk about building a home for your spirit. The home for your heart is primarily concerned with the first two—romantic relationships and friendships.

THINKING LIKE GOLDILOCKS

Thinking like Goldilocks in your relationships means balancing the time you spend alone with the time you spend with others. It's not healthy to be alone all the time, nor is it healthy never to be alone. If you're married, finding balance also means having enough time alone with your spouse while not neglecting other friendships. Again, it's not good for the marriage if you never spend time with just your spouse, but it's also not healthy if you never spend time with other couples and friends. Time spent with other friends but without your spouse should be kept to a minimum. There's nothing wrong with the occasional girls' night or guys' camping trip, but if you find yourself going in different directions on the weekend nights or taking separate vacations, you're looking for trouble. Another aspect of finding balance is negotiating your own needs versus the needs of others. If you always

think of yourself first, it will be harder to find friends. On the other hand, if you never attend to your own needs, people may not respect you and may take advantage of you. The trick is to find that happy medium where you are unselfish yet not allowing yourself to be a doormat.

DAFFY DUCK AND THE GIANT SNOWBALL

I remember as a kid watching Saturday morning cartoons—this was before there were whole cable channels devoted to cartoons. There was nothing funnier than when Wile E. Coyote fell off a cliff and kept falling and getting smaller and smaller until you couldn't see him anymore, but then you saw that little cloud of dust when he hit the bottom of the canyon. Even though I knew it was coming, it cracked me up every time. I also loved to see Daffy Duck trip and fall down a snow-covered hill. He would become covered with snow, and as he rolled down the hill, he became enveloped in a giant snowball that got bigger and bigger as it rolled. We even have an expression for this phenomenon. We say something "snowballed" until it was out of control. You get the idea—the farther the snowball rolls down the hill, the bigger it gets, and the harder it would be to stop it, let alone reverse its direction.

Relationships are like that snowball. Once they gain a certain amount of momentum, it's very hard to turn them around. A relationship can go in one of two directions, like that snowball can roll down one side of the hill or the other. And it all depends on something we've already mentioned, something that was very important to Jesus—forgiveness. In other words, it all depends on your ability to apologize and to give and receive forgiveness. If you're in a relationship where it's hard to apologize when you're wrong, or if you apologize and the other person refuses to forgive—giving you a hard time about it and then bringing it up again later—then it just gets harder and harder to apologize, and it gets harder and harder for the other person to forgive. It's like the snowball is rolling down the wrong side of the hill, and it's very hard to stop it and turn it around. We call this a vicious cycle. Refusing to apologize leads to refusal to forgive, and refusing to forgive leads to an even firmer refusal to apologize. This leads to defensiveness, blaming, and criticism. This in turn leads to withdrawal, distance, lack of intimacy and lack of respect, and eventually resentment, which is poison to the relationship.

On the other hand, if you can both apologize and forgive easily, then the snowball rolls in the right direction. Being quick to apologize leads to real forgiveness; real forgiveness makes a person even quicker to apologize; this leads to reconciliation, which is like glue to the relationship. In any relationship, but especially in a marriage, it has to be safe to admit you are wrong and apologize. To be safe means that you know when you apologize, your apology will be accepted without conditions or criticism, and you will be forgiven. If a relationship is safe in this way, then chances are that relationship is a good home for your heart, because you can feel secure knowing that you can be yourself. The relationship itself is not threatened by conflict. This is the kind of security we all hope to find, the kind that brings peace.

As we look closer at building a home for your heart, notice that there are sections of the next chapter specifically for single and married people. I encourage everyone to read both sections, since there are things to be learned from each kind of relationship. Whether you are single or married, reading the other section can give you information you can apply to your friendships. If you are dating, engaged, or "engaged to be engaged," it is also a good idea to read the section for married couples and apply those principles to your relationship now. If you are single, read the section for married people to think about the kind of person you may be looking for and what kind of marriage relationship you want. If you are single but committed to a celibate lifestyle, such as in a religious community, or if you live with one or more friends or roommates, then read the section for married people with an eye toward applying the principles to the people with whom you live.

On the other hand, if you are not married, but you live with someone who is preventing your house or apartment from being a good home for your body by causing you stress, you may have to move and/or get a new housemate. This demonstrates how the homes are interrelated and how the home for your heart (relationships) affects the home for your body (where you live). When there is no religious vow holding you together, sometimes it's best to admit it's not working out and move on.

Although most people will be surrounded by multiple relationships and even separate groups of friends who don't necessarily know each other, I prefer to think of all of these significant relationships collectively as the one home for the heart. This may or may not include a spouse. But rather than imagining each relationship as a separate home for your heart, consider that all of your important relationships combine to make up the one home for your heart. In reality, no one relationship can provide everything you need for a home for your heart, not even a spouse, but the combination of all of your important relationships can give you what you need to be happy.

As you read the next chapter, think about what you're looking for in your relationships and think about what may be missing. In the reflection chapter, you will have the opportunity to make some notes about what you need to continue to build the home for your heart.

11

A **Home for Your Heart**: Where You Find Love

PEOPLE WITH GLASS HEARTS shouldn't throw stones.

Like the other homes, what we are looking for in a home for our heart is a home of security and peace. Therefore, a good home for your heart is a relationship (or combination of relationships) in which it is safe to be yourself—in other words, safe to be imperfect, to be wrong, and to make mistakes. It must be safe to apologize without the fear of being made to feel inferior and without the fear that apologizing will make things worse rather than better. A good home for your heart brings a feeling of unconditional acceptance, which leads to security and peace of mind. It is also where gratitude is felt and expressed through acts of service and shared activities that bring enjoyment.

It is easy to see, therefore, that building a home for your heart is not only up to you but depends on the cooperation of the other people in your life. This also means that you are helping to build the heart homes of your friends and loved ones. It's a two-way street, and that is never more true than when it comes to establishing peace and security through unconditional acceptance.

In other words, if you want your friends and significant other to accept you as you are, you will need to learn to accept them as they are and help them build a safe home for their hearts by being quick to accept their apologies and quick to forgive them. When you make it safe for them to apologize, you are indirectly making it safer for you as well, since it will motivate them to be more willing to apologize and accept your apologies.

IF YOU'RE SINGLE...

Finding a significant other is much harder than just finding a new friend. This is because the risk of heartbreak is so much greater, and so people are more guarded. Therefore, meeting the right person is often outside your control. You can't make that meeting happen, primarily because you don't know who that right person is yet. And even if you do find someone who seems right, you soon learn what Bonnie Raitt sang about and what Jim Carrey's character, Bruce, learned in the 2003 film, *Bruce Almighty*: you can't make someone love you. "You can't hurry love," to quote another song title. You can't rush it and you can't force it—but there is something you can do—in fact, you're doing it right now. You can work on improving and ordering your life so that you become more attractive to high-quality, potential mates.

What this means is that if you are looking for the home for your heart in a significant other, you may have to work on the other four homes first. But I would not be at all surprised if you found that significant other in the process—*because of the process*—of working on the other four homes. So rather than focusing on the other person who is out there somewhere, you're going to focus on yourself and focus on making yourself more desirable. Think about it: you're reading this book because you want less chaos and more peace in your life. Any potential mate out there also wants less chaos in his or her life, so if your life is chaotic, then you're not going to be what he or she is looking for. But if you can bring order and peace into your life, then it's a whole different story. So be patient, and just keep your eyes open while you work on your homes. Of course, you can build the home for your heart right now by looking for new friendships or devoting time and energy to the friendships you already have.

Another reason not to rush the process is that in doing so, we usually make mistakes. Bad choices often come from trying to make lifelong decisions when you're too young or when you feel pressured by the passage of time or other outside forces. The truth is, you may have to get

to know yourself better before you can know who is right for you. In fact, many people who marry young end up choosing a mate who reminds them of (and is subconsciously meant to replace) a parent or other significant person from their childhood. This is called *transference*, and some people actually marry someone who has the same negative character traits as a person from their childhood, only to remember later why they wanted to move out of the house! Even worse, some people choose a mate with a problem that is familiar from their childhood, subconsciously hoping to fix in adulthood the problem that could not be fixed in childhood. Or they hope to gain love and acceptance from someone who reminds them of a person who failed to show them love in their childhood. These kinds of transference are not necessarily fatal to a marriage, but they will probably require counseling to turn the marriage into a safe home for the heart. If you are currently dating or engaged, you are encouraged to use the reflection questions in the next chapter to ask yourself whether transference might have been part of your attraction to your significant other. In any case, the point is that even though you may feel pressure to find a significant other soon, you will be better off if you don't try to rush it or force it. It is just another one of life's little ironies: if you chase after Ms. or Mr. Right, you will only be trying to force yourself to be blind to the ways that Ms. or Mr. Wrong are wrong for you. Or if you marry Ms. or Mr. Wrong hoping to change her or him into Ms. or Mr. Right, you will only be disappointed. Instead, stop thinking of yourself as a treasure hunter and start thinking of yourself as the treasure. Then Ms. or Mr. Right will find you!

If you are reading this book thinking that you are lonely, that you have no significant other and no important friends to share your life with, I promised I would give you some ideas for ways out of loneliness. Since you can't rush the process of finding a mate, the first thing to do is work on making some new friends. Here quantity is the key, since you will need to meet a lot of people to find a few close friends. Again, don't think of them as potential mates, since they will sense that and put their guard up. You are only trying to make friends. If one turns into something more, that would be fine, but if you try to force it, you will certainly push people away. In fact, at first you should focus on making *groups* of friends, not individual friends, since there is safety in numbers. If you're shy, it may be a bit harder, but don't worry. This is not about trying to be someone you're not. You don't have to be the life of the party. In fact, I don't recommend parties or bars at all, because the music is usually too loud to talk.

As I said earlier, getting your life in order will make you more attractive to other people. That applies to potential friends as well as people you might want to date. So the strategy here is to work on building your other four homes and to look for new friends along the way. While you're building the home for your hands, make friends at work. Start having lunch with people. Help others with their work. Go out of your way to serve them by getting them coffee or something else they need. Get a few of your coworkers to go out together after work. While you're building the home for your body, make friends with your neighbors. Organize a block party or multi-home rummage sale (this will dovetail nicely with de-cluttering your house). If you find you want to move, take into account the neighborhood or apartment building you move into and look for potential friends. While you're building the home for your mind, join a gym or sports league and make friends there. Take tennis or karate lessons and make friends in the class. Take an art or craft class like painting, pottery, or scrapbooking. And while you're building the home for your spirit, make friends at church by getting more involved there. Volunteer for something you haven't done before. Chances are the church already has a social group for people your age (whatever that is). By putting yourself in these group situations, you will grow as a person and meet other people who are also growing.

IF YOU'RE MARRIED...

If you are married, stop for a moment right now and thank God for your spouse. This person is (or should be) your best friend, closest companion, and trusted confidant. Even if the marriage is not perfect, and even if you don't feel very thankful right now, try to think about the good things that your marriage brings you and thank God for those things. Try to remember what attracted you to your spouse when you first met. Why did you fall in love? In what ways is your spouse the same as he or she was back then? Thank God for these things.

Remember that your marriage is your primary vocation. It takes precedence over your career, even over other members of your family. Only your relationship with God is more important than your marriage. Therefore your spouse must be the number one person in your life, even over your parents, even over your own children. You might think that the children should come first, but in reality, the best thing you can do for your children is to make your spouse your first priority. That way they will grow up with security and peace, which will give them a healthy self-assurance. Your marriage and your home is the primary place where you live the values of God's kingdom. If you're not doing it there, whatever happens outside the home is set on a shaky foundation. You and your spouse are a team in building the foundation for everything you do when you are not together. Your spouse is also one of the primary ways that God loves you, and whenever you love and forgive your spouse, you are a channel of God's love and grace to him or her. God is actually using your

spouse to love you and using you to love your spouse—if you let him.

In a previous job, I was in charge of marriage preparation ministries for a large church. One of the things I had to do was meet with all of the engaged couples who were planning a wedding at the church. Whenever I stood in front of a room full of engaged couples, I always told them this: There are three ways to do marriage. There's the traditional way, the modern way, and the right way. The traditional way to do marriage is what I call "Master and Servant." One person, usually the man, takes the role of master. He makes all the important decisions, and the other person goes along with them. That way of doing marriage lasted for many centuries, but once divorce became easier, it became clear that everyone wasn't happy. The person in the servant role often got tired of being less than a full partner in the relationship and eventually wanted out. The modern way of doing marriage is an attempt at equality, but I call it "Master and Master." It's two people fighting for control. Two people who want to be master of their own world, unwilling to give too much for fear of losing everything. And the divorce rate keeps going up. By now you see where this is going. The right way to do marriage is what I call "Servant and Servant." It's two people serving each other. Since both are in the servant role, neither takes advantage of the other's servanthood. This is the only way of doing marriage that combines equality with security.

In fact, the Servant-Servant marriage is exactly what the apostle Paul was talking about in his letter to the Ephesians. In chapter 5, Paul wrote, "Wives, be subject to your husbands as you are to the Lord....Husbands, love your wives, just as Christ loved the church and gave himself up for her....In the same way, husbands should love their wives as they do their own bodies. He who loves his wife loves himself" (Ephesians 5:22–28). As you can imagine, Paul gets a lot of criticism for those words. If one fails to read it carefully, it can sound like the traditional Master and Servant type of marriage, with the wife taking the servant role. But reading it that way misses the next part, where Paul tells husbands to love their wives, "just as Christ loved the church"—in other words, with a self-sacrificing love. Paul isn't advocating a Master and Servant marriage; he's advocating a Servant-Servant marriage, so in fact he was ahead of his time. He's just using two different concepts to speak of servanthood to men and women. To the women he's saying, respect your husbands, because they need to feel respected. To the men he's saying, love your wives, because they need to feel loved. In truth, both men and women want both love and respect, but Paul is simply saying that in a marriage, selfishness is not the way. Selfless service is the way.

The bottom line here is that in order for your marriage to be a good home for your heart, it has to be a relationship of mutual service. Ironically, you can't get what you want by trying to get what you want. However, you will find that your needs are met when you try to meet your partner's needs. Demanding what you want never works. All you can really do is tell your partner how to love you, listen when your partner tells you how to love him or her, and then try to do what he or she needs. If you can do this, you will help that snowball to roll in the right direction. If you refuse to do this, you will push the snowball down the wrong side of the hill. But the truth is, not getting what you want is better for you than getting what you want by coercion, guilt, or manipulation, since if you get what you want in this way, it always comes with a side order of resentment.

Therefore, the key ingredient in the Servant-Servant marriage is humility. Humility is the opposite of taking an attitude of entitlement and making yourself the center of attention. It's the opposite of focusing on getting what you want. Humility is focusing on giving the other person what he or she wants—and guess what? That will make him or her *want* to give you what you want. Real humility comes from gratitude—counting your blessings and being thankful for what you have—and from admitting that you are not perfect, either. Most people are too satisfied with themselves, as if they don't need to grow, but they are unsatisfied with what they have, as if they deserve better. Humility means learning to be satisfied with what you have, while being unsatisfied with the way you are, so that you are willing to try to grow.

THE JOB DESCRIPTION OF A MARRIED PERSON

There are two lies that the world wants you to believe. If you believe them, they can kill your marriage. Lie number one is: *True love is a happy ending.* This lie attempts to get you to believe that love is something you arrive at or achieve, and once you reach that point, everything is smooth sailing. My wife and I like the 1999 film, *Notting Hill,* starring Hugh Grant and Julia Roberts. It's a fun romantic comedy that's surprisingly enjoyable, even for the guy who prefers movies with explosions. But as much as I like this film, I recognize that it's perpetuating the lie. The problem is that the movie ends at the beginning. What I mean is that the story ends with the two stars happily married—a happy ending—as if all the conflict is now over. But the reality is that this is just the beginning of the their relationship, and if this were a real couple, there would certainly be more conflict, negotiations, arguments, misunderstandings, harsh words, and apologies to come.

The truth is that true love is not a happy ending. Marriage, like life, is a journey—not a destination. In other words, it's not a static state of being you achieve and then that's it. Marriage is not like a mansion that is grand and beautiful, but once it's built, it's done and you just live in it. Marriage is more like an oak tree that continues to grow. In fact, if it's not growing, it's dying. Keeping this in mind will help you deal with change over time, because change will come, whether you want it to or not.

The other lie that the world wants you to believe is: *You are now the person you were meant to be.* In other words, you don't need to grow or change. In fact, we have been conditioned to fear change, as if it's the loss of some part of who we are. The truth is that you are not perfect—none of us are—and there is room for growth and improvement. To realize our potential, we have to be willing to change and grow. In order to do this, we have to recognize our unchangeable identity as children of God, made in the image of God, so that we will feel free to change some behaviors and mature in character without feeling like we have to become someone else. Then we can allow our relationship with God to help us mature into the likeness of Christ. So change is not loss; it's gain. But in a relationship, especially a marriage, we often fear change (either in ourselves or in the other person), because we are afraid that the relationship will change. It's going to change anyway —the question is just whether it will change in the right direction (grow) or change in the wrong direction.

The reality is that men usually don't change

as much as their wives want them to, and women usually change more than their husbands want them to. This is because women marry the potential, and men marry the ideal. When Billy Joel sang, "Just the Way You Are," most men could relate—in fact, they might prefer it if the song were called, "Just the Way You WERE," and if the lyrics went something like this: "Don't go changing…I liked you just the way you were when we met…" But of course, that's not a realistic expectation. Everyone will change just from the passing of time, but more than that, everyone *should* grow throughout life. Therefore, part of your job description as a married person is to accept your spouse as he or she is right now and commit to sticking together, even if he or she never changes. But you must also allow him or her to grow and commit to sticking together, even if he or she should change. Encourage healthy change and growth that is self-initiated. You can't change your spouse, but you can encourage growth when the desire comes from him or her. Ironically, people only feel free to grow when they feel safe in the knowledge that they are accepted as they are. In other words, it's only safe to improve when it's safe to be imperfect. If you try to force your spouse to change, you will only change your spouse into a resentful person. **Accept your spouse as he or she is, but enable healthy growth.**

Growth includes spiritual growth. We'll cover this more when we look at building the home for your spirit, but part of your job as a spouse is to encourage spiritual growth. Motivate each other to get to church (not by nagging, but by example), and pray for your spouse. In many marriages, there is one person who wants to go to church more than the other. That's normal. I call it the dragger and the dragee. One person drags the other to church. Maybe you're the dragger. You get up on Sunday and make sure everyone is ready to get out the door on time. Maybe you even remind your spouse on Saturday, "Don't forget we're going to the eleven o'clock tomorrow." Or maybe you're the dragee. You would really rather sleep late or have a more relaxing morning most Sundays, and you're tired of feeling a little guilty about it, but you realize it's important. At least it's important to your partner. Fair enough. But each of you is responsible for helping the other be the best they can be and for bringing out the best in each other. That means not criticizing or trying to change your partner if he or she is naturally the dragee, but it also means not trying to talk your spouse out of going to church if you are the dragee. If you can resist the temptation to enable spiritual laziness, and if you can try to be strong for each other, you can help bring out the best in each other. God put the two of you together to help each other cultivate good habits, not enable each other's worst habits. Therefore, any time there is a conflict, a negotiation, or a decision to be made, you should ask yourself, **What course of action will bring out the best in my spouse?**

Not all couples find it easy to pray together. If you are not comfortable praying out loud together, pray together silently. If you're not comfortable praying together at all, at least pray *for* each other, and tell your spouse you're praying for him or her. Share with each other things you can be praying for. In time, you may become more comfortable praying together. But even if you don't, all of this will work to your benefit, as it strengthens the relationship and increases the level of happiness in your home. It's harder to be in conflict if you are sincerely praying for each other. **So pray for each other.**

We've already seen how important it is to get into a positive cycle of apology and forgiveness. This is very important in a marriage because even though you are trying to bring out the best in each other, the fact that you live together means that you will undoubtedly also see each other at your worst. Mistakes will be made, and apologies will be necessary; there's no way around it. Therefore it is extremely important that you be willing to apologize, but it is perhaps even more important that you be willing to forgive when your partner apologizes. That means when your spouse says, "I'm sorry," you can't come back with, "Well, you SHOULD be sorry..." and then proceed to make the person feel even worse. It

also means once forgiven, it's forgotten, so no fair bringing up old mistakes as part of a new argument. You have to let the last be the past, and never let the sun go down on your anger (Ephesians 4:26). Every day *must be* a new beginning with a clean slate. Otherwise, you will find yourself rolling down the wrong side of the hill trying to stop a runaway snowball. **Be quick to apologize, and make it safe for your spouse to apologize by being quick to forgive and forget.**

Being quick to apologize also means being willing to admit when you are wrong. This is hard for many of us. My maternal grandfather used to have a saying, which I like to repeat when I'm feeling mischievous: "I was only wrong once....It was the time I thought I was wrong, but it turned out I was right." We all think we're right, and to be proven wrong is something most people avoid at all costs, to the point where some are willing to live in denial rather than face the truth. We want to be right, often because we think people won't respect us if we admit we're wrong. But actually the opposite is true. People respect you more if you can admit when you're wrong. Once when I was using the Dustbuster, I knocked over a champagne glass. My first thought was to blame it on my wife: "Why did you put that champagne glass there?!" In my mind, for a split second, I actually believed that my wife would respect me more if she thought knocking over the glass was not my fault. So I was tempted to blame it on her, to retain her respect. I know it sounds stupid when you see it in print, but we often reason like this in the heat of the moment. Thankfully, in that situation, I stopped myself from saying the first thing that came to mind and took responsibility for the accident. My wife was still a little annoyed with me, but not nearly as much as she would have been if I had tried to blame it on her. In other situations where I have blamed something on her that was not her fault, it became an argument. But this time, by admitting I was wrong and apologizing, I avoided the argument, and the day was not ruined by negative emotions. This just proves the point that people will respect you more if you can take responsibility for your actions and apologize. So do it—**admit when you're wrong, and you will create an environment where it is safe for your spouse to do the same.**

But what if you're not wrong? In those cases where you are sure you're right, you will have to figure out how far you can go in pressing your point before the disagreement becomes an argument or before the argument becomes a fight. Once you cross that line, the damage is done. Learn to give up before you cross that line. I think about it this way: It's better to be wrong and sleep in your own bed than to be right and sleep on the couch. You already know that nobody wins these arguments. If you press your point far enough, one of two things happens.

Either you prove that you are right, and then your spouse is embarrassed, or it comes to a stalemate, and your spouse thinks you're stubborn and pigheaded. It's a lose-lose proposition. In the end, it's more important to be on the same side as your spouse than it is to be right. I've learned in my marriage that I would rather be wrong with my wife than right alone. Sometimes those are your only two options. Therefore, you should never take a side with anyone against your spouse. Not your friends, not your parents, not your kids, no one. If there is a real issue where you believe your spouse is wrong, stick together until you can discuss it in private. Otherwise, you've created a situation that is not a safe home for your spouse's heart. Remember that your marriage is your primary vocation, and your spouse is number one—not to mention the one you will go home with—so never take sides against your spouse. **Always be on the same side as your spouse, even if he or she is wrong.**

But sometimes your spouse is right. Chances are if your spouse keeps bringing up the same issue(s), there is probably some truth there. Don't be afraid of the truth—it will set you free (see John 8:32). Rather than dismiss the repetition as "nagging," learn to listen to those recurring issues. They are not criticisms of you, they are your spouse's attempts at telling you how to love and serve him or her. If they are ignored, they will erode your spouse's happiness. Most likely the issues have something to do with behavior. But remember, your behavior is not your identity, so you are free to change your behavior without having to become someone you're not. Don't forget that you are helping to build the home for your spouse's heart, and learning to make your relationship more loving and more serving is the way to do that. And if you think about it, changing your behavior in a way that makes your spouse happy is not only an act of unselfish love, it is also self-improvement. So that's a win-win solution to a "nagging" problem. If the home for your heart is one in which it is safe to be yourself, safe to be imperfect, and safe to be wrong, then it is also one in which it is safe to change and grow. If you don't feel that your marriage is this kind of home for your heart right now, start by making sure you create this kind of home for your spouse's heart, and that will motivate him or her to do the same for you. Eventually both of you will learn to serve each other and communicate your needs in ways that don't sound so much like nagging. **Be willing to change your behavior when it will demonstrate love for your spouse.**

Since your marriage is your primary relationship, it deserves your time. Time is like the currency of love, and making an investment of time in your marriage will always pay off. Be intentional about putting your spouse on the calendar. This will communicate that he or she is a priority. On the other hand, the reality is

that you will probably spend more time with coworkers than you will with your spouse, and that's just the way it is when you have to earn a living. So resist the temptation to use time as a measuring stick. Don't assume that the amount of time a person spends on one thing or another is an absolute reflection of that person's priorities. Just make time for each other, and tell each other when you feel you're not getting enough time. Remember that your spouse is not a mind reader, so the only way to communicate what you need is to clearly explain it, without accusations that will put your partner on the defensive. Also remember to balance time spent alone, time spent alone with each other, and time spent with friends.

An important part of the time you spend together will include talking and especially listening. As I said in the section on building a home for your body, your house has to be a place where each person can vent when you need to. That means each of you has to be available for the other if one of you needs to talk about things (even things you don't both care about). Usually one or both partners need to debrief at the end of each day, and that helps put the things that cause stress aside so the person can relax. However, the reality is that in many marriages, one person needs to talk more than the other. One person may need to talk about the day, the conversations and conflicts, joys and frustrations. Until it's talked out, the person can't relax. But that person might be married to someone who doesn't need to talk about his or her day. In fact, some people don't *want* to talk about their day. In order to relax, this type of person needs to put it out of his or her mind completely. The important thing to realize is that neither way is wrong; it just depends on a person's personality. Being a servant to your spouse means being available to listen if that's what your partner needs, even if it's not what you need. Isn't this what you would have done when you were dating or when you were newlyweds? You would have given your undivided attention and listened unselfishly. So why did you stop treating each other the way you did when you were dating? **And what would it be like if you made a pact to act like newlyweds forever?** Remember, real listening means you're not trying to think of what you're going to say next while the other person is talking. Most of the time, the person is not looking for advice, so just listening is enough. Resist the temptation to give advice unless he or she asks for it (this one is hard for me, but I'm working on it). **Listen unselfishly, and don't give advice unless asked.**

It's also important to give your spouse a sounding board for plans and dreams. Since the two of you are going to spend your future together, you need to share dreams for the future with each other. However, dreams are just that, and a person has to be free to say things out loud that may never come true. Therefore,

keep in mind that a person may talk about something just to hear how it sounds when said out loud. Think of it as brainstorming. Try not to be threatened by any dreams that catch you off guard or don't seem to fit with your plans. Don't be a dream killer by reacting negatively to something that is only hypothetical. Your job is to encourage your spouse's dreams, and by doing so, you enhance his or her sense of hope for the future. Even if the things he or she shares will never come true, it's not your place to say that. Let things take their natural course, and you will be the hero who builds your spouse's hopes. **Don't be a dream killer—encourage your spouse's hopes and dreams.**

Finally, if your home is a source of stress, and you think your spouse is part of the reason, take the initiative to fulfill *your* job description and lead by example. Remember that your spouse can't read your mind, so tell him or her in plain terms (without accusations) what you need to feel loved. Share how *you* feel rather than focusing on your spouse, and be careful not to put it in terms that make it sound like it's your spouse's fault. Resist the temptation to blame or shame. Don't speak in absolutes ("You always…" "You never…"). And *never* embarrass or humiliate your spouse in front of other people. Did I say *never*? I meant NEVER. Also let your spouse tell you what he or she needs, and really listen to the answer. I highly recommend the book, *The Five*

Love Languages, by Gary Chapman. This book goes into detail about the fact that what you need may not be the same things your spouse needs, and it will help you learn to give each other what each one needs. Every married couple should read this book. Once you understand Chapman's concept of the love languages and the love tank, it will change your life and your relationship. If that doesn't help enough, then it's time to see a marriage counselor. But remember, there is no shame in going to couple's therapy. It is not a failure to admit you need help. Don't be like a dentist who tries to drill his own teeth.

BE WHAT YOU HOPE TO FIND

Whether you're single or married, if you are looking for more or better relationships, you can't get there by changing other people. You can only get there by improving yourself. In other words, if you want to have friends, you have to be a friend. If you want to find a lover, you have to learn to be a lover. It's ironic, but you already know it's true—being selfish about it will actually work against you and drive people away. But by being unselfish and focusing on others, you will become more attractive to them. Being unselfish is really the best thing you can do for yourself.

There was a time when I worked in marketing for a major credit card company. We were launching a new platinum card, and we were having a brainstorming session. In a discussion about customer service, someone brought up the concept of the Golden Rule. "Do to others as you would have them do to you" (Matthew 7:12). Then someone in the group (I wish I could claim it was me, but it wasn't) said, "How about a *Platinum Rule*?" Rather than treating people the way *you* want to be treated, treat people the way *they* want to be treated. What a concept! Unfortunately, the idea never made its way into the marketing department (let alone customer service) of the credit card in question, but what if we applied the Platinum Rule to our relationships? Too often we assume everyone wants to be treated the same way we do. That may not be the case. Being a friend or a spouse means listening to the other person so you know how *they* want to be treated. Then it means going out of your way to treat them that way.

Almost everyone is familiar with the Scripture verse that says, "God is love" (1 John 4:8). But it's probably so familiar that it's lost some of its meaning. God is love because God invented love, and love is God's expression of himself. Since we are created in the image of God, we also express ourselves through love, and in fact, we have a built-in need for love and acceptance. That's because love is a two-way street. It's the gift you have to give away to keep. Love is not just an emotion, because unexpressed love is not really love. As DC Talk once rapped, "Love is a Verb." It is not a passive feeling, but it is action. It is an act of will that comes from a rational decision. Since we are made in the image of a rational, active, and loving God, real love expressed between people is also rational and active. In Paul's famous "love chapter," 1 Corinthians 13, he described what real love is like and what we have to be like in order to show love and to receive love. I encourage you to look this chapter up in your Bible—you'll notice that Paul is describing loves in terms of action. I have paraphrased the passage below to make it apply more specifically to relationships. As you read this, think about your relationships and how you can be more intentional about making your relationships into channels of God's love and into good homes for the hearts of you and your friends and loved ones.

*If I can speak eloquently but use that gift
to be hurtful, it is worthless.
If I understand human nature and
psychology but use that to manipulate
or humiliate, it is worthless.*

*If I am generous toward strangers but mean
to the ones closest to me, I am a hypocrite.
If I give so much of myself to things
outside the home that there's nothing left
at the end of the day,
then all that hard work is for nothing*

*Love is patient.
Love is gentle.*

*Love is trusting, always assuming
the best of the other.
Love is a servant to the other.*

*Love seeks the best for the other
before the self.
Love gives what the other needs
before asserting its own rights.*

*Love always gives the other
the benefit of the doubt.
Love is forgiving, always willing to forget
the mistakes of the past and start again
with a clean slate.*

*Love is always truthful and not afraid
of the truth or living in denial of the truth.
Love sees anything done for the other
as a labor of love.*

*Love has a positive attitude and remains
optimistic about the future.
Love never gives up*

*When I was a child, I was the center
of attention and others catered to me.
I thought love should be easy.*

*Now that I am an adult, I have to admit
that it's not all about me,
and that love requires initiative and action.*

*But at least I know that love is worth the risk,
because the love that we share will last
forever.*

12

Reflection on the **Home for Your Heart**

WHERE DID I COME FROM?

What qualities or attributes of your parents or childhood caregivers would you like to imitate?

_____

_____

What qualities or attributes of your parents or caregivers would you like to find in your spouse?

_____

_____

What qualities or attributes of your parents or childhood caregivers would you like to avoid?

_____

_____

What is keeping you from emulating the best qualities of your parents or caregivers?

_____

_____

Are there people in your life now who exhibit the worst qualities of your parents or caregivers?

_____

_____

_____

IF YOU'RE SINGLE...

What characteristics are you looking for in a significant other? It's OK to make a list! _____

_____

What characteristics do you want to avoid in a spouse? _____

_____

Are you happy with the amount of time you spend alone? _____

Are you happy with the amount of time you spend with friends?_____

What steps would you have to take (or groups to join) to make some new friends? _____

_____

IF YOU'RE MARRIED...

Let's begin by reviewing the job description of a husband or wife:

1. Accept your spouse as he or she is, but enable and encourage healthy growth.
2. Always choose the course of action that will bring out the best in your spouse.
3. Encourage spiritual growth by praying with and/or for each other.
4. Be quick to apologize, and make it safe for your spouse to apologize by being quick to forgive and forget.
5. Always be on the same side as your spouse, even if he or she is wrong.
6. Be willing to change your behavior when it will demonstrate love for your spouse.
7. Listen unselfishly, but don't give advice unless asked.
8. Don't be a dream killer—encourage your spouse's hopes and dreams.
9. Make a pact with your spouse to act like newlyweds forever!
10. Never forget that you are helping each other build the homes for your body and heart.

If your marriage were a snowball, would it be rolling in the right direction, or are you in a vicious cycle?

_____

Do you find it difficult to apologize or to give in? _____

Do you make it safe for your spouse to apologize to you? _____

Is it safe to be wrong in your marriage, or do you worry about the stability of the relationship? _____

_____

Do you ever take sides with anyone against your spouse? _____

Do you ever humiliate your spouse in front of others or create conflict in public? _____

Which of the three kinds of marriage do you think you have? Master-Servant? Master-Master?

Servant-Servant? _____

What could you do to be more of a servant to your spouse? _____

_____

Do you feel that you and your spouse accept each other as you are? _____

Do you feel that you and your spouse encourage each other to grow in healthy ways? (Resist the temptation to point fingers; evaluate yourself first.) _____

Are you happy with the amount of time spent alone with your spouse? _____

Are you happy with the amount of time spent with your spouse and other friends? _____

Do you think your spouse is happy with the amount of time you spend together? _____

_____

BEING A FRIEND

What are you looking for in your relationships? _____

_____

_____

Would you rather have a lot of friends or a few very close friends? _____

Are you happy with the number of friends you have? _____

Who are your friends? Make a list: _____

_____

Who are your *best* friends, your "inner circle"? _____

_____

Do you think you are in their inner circle, too? Which ones would count you among their best friends?

_____

List some things you can do to show your friends that you appreciate them. _____

_____

BEING GOLDILOCKS

Have you found the right balance of taking care of your own needs and serving others?_____

_____

Honesty time... Are you too selfish? _____

Are you sometimes taken advantage of? _____

_____

Evaluation

Which do you think applies to you? Circle all the statements that sound like your situation right now. Then choose one of the categories below:

Rebuild: You feel alone. If you are single, you feel you lack close friendships that give you a sense of peace and security. If you are married, the marriage does not feel safe, and there is growing distance and resentment. You may be in a vicious cycle of refusal to apologize and refusal to forgive.

Remodel: You spend too much time alone. If you are single, you often wait for others to call you to do something and find yourself disappointed when no one calls. If you are married, the marriage seems secure, but there are some problems that get in the way of your happiness. Maybe it feels like you and your spouse do not spend enough time together.

Redecorate: You are generally satisfied with the people in your life, but you could organize your time better to spend an appropriate amount of time with them. Maybe you could work on your balance of taking care of self and others. If you are married, maybe you need to work on one or more of the points in the job description.

Appreciate: You have a good home for your heart. Your relationships combine to fulfill your need to feel wanted and appreciated. Your relationships feel secure and bring you peace and happiness. You can be thankful for this area of life. Say a prayer of thanksgiving to God for your significant other and/or friends and for the home for your heart.

13

Kosher Bacon: The Paradox of the Christian Faith

I HAVE A PERSONALITY that doesn't tolerate mystery very well. I want to get to the bottom of every question, and I want concrete answers. That's the reason I started studying theology. I came to believe that there was no more important subject to study, and I wanted to know the answers to all the questions. The problem is that when you seriously study the Scriptures and traditions of the faith, and when you think you have finally gotten to the bottom of the mystery, what you often find is a deeper mystery. For example, if you want to understand God, you could study the Scriptures, and you could study the way Christian theologians have historically interpreted the Scriptures, but the best you will do is begin to understand how the Church has *described* God. You may learn to understand the ways that others have tried to understand God, but even the best minds that the Church has ever produced would admit that you will never understand God as God really is. You can only understand the ways that God has revealed himself, and the ways believers have interpreted that revelation. The truth is that truth itself is a bottomless well. You will never master it, and

you will never finish studying it. That doesn't mean we shouldn't try. It just means that we have to approach the study of divine things with a significant amount of humility.

Some early theologians even claimed that you could never really say what God *is*, you can only say what God *is not*, and by saying what God *is not*, you can begin to contemplate (though never fully understand) what God *is*. For example, God is not fickle or capricious. God does not change. Therefore God is trustworthy. But these early theologians would have said that this is about as far as you can go. You can know enough about God to put your trust in him, but you could never know enough to allow you to begin to think you've got him figured out. After all, he is God, and you are not. In fact, that pretty much sums up all of Hebrew wisdom literature. God is God, and you are not. God is wise, and you are not. God's foolishness is wiser than the wisdom of humans, which means that sometimes the wisdom of God seems like foolishness to those who take pride in their own wisdom. There is a paradox here, a mystery that seems like a contradiction, and yet it is true. The paradox is this: if you think you are wise, then you're foolish. But if you humbly admit that you are not wise—now that's wisdom! (See Proverbs 9:10).

The whole of the Christian faith is built on this paradox. Ultimately, we have to trust in a God we could never fully understand. But if you think about it, if you could completely understand God, wouldn't that make you at least as smart as God, maybe more so? Why would I want to put my trust in someone who is less wise and less complicated than myself? It might make it possible for me to understand him, but it would disqualify him as a higher power. No, we can put our trust in God precisely *because* he is beyond our understanding. In fact, if you look at our faith, you soon discover that it is a series of paradoxes through and through. And only by embracing the mystery and by letting go of the need to have all the answers can we truly entrust ourselves to God.

THE ANCIENT ONE IS DOING SOMETHING NEW

God is called the Ancient One (see Daniel 7:13), because he is eternal and has always existed. The Scriptures assure us that God is immutable, or unchanging (see Malachi 3:6; James 1:17; Hebrews 13:8). But even though God is unchanging, God is not just a stagnant, impersonal force. Rather God is a personal (and by that we mean relational) divine being who is eternally active and who continues to be active in human history. The Old Testament prophets knew that God was not finished with his creative activity. Isaiah predicted that God's people would sing a new song (see Isaiah 42:10; Psalm 33, 40, 96, 98, 144, 149). Jeremiah predicted a new covenant (see Jeremiah 31:31–34).

This new covenant would be a covenant of forgiveness, which was made necessary because humanity had used its free will to bring evil into the world. In a way, the presence of evil created a problem for God. God had to enforce the consequences of sin or his justice would be compromised (Romans 6:23). On the other hand, God's mercy meant that he had compassion for his creatures and wanted to release them from the consequences of their sin (2 Peter 3:9). The apparent conflict of God's justice and his mercy created the problem: only humanity could atone for the sins of humanity, but since all humans are burdened with sin, humans are incapable of atoning for sin. The solution to the problem was something new, and it was yet another paradox: the sinless human known as Jesus Christ.

Jesus himself is undoubtedly the most profound paradox of the Christian faith. He is the divine human, born of the virgin mother, born to become the crucified Messiah. All of these concepts would seem like insurmountable contradictions to most of the people of Jesus' time, both Jews and Gentiles (1 Corinthians

1:23). Nevertheless, Jesus is immanent transcendence, "God is with us" (Matthew 1:23). Both his birth and his death are examples of the previously unthinkable paradox of divine humility, as he was born a helpless baby and eventually suffered on the cross (see Philippians 2:5–8). And while most Jews believed that being executed as a criminal would have disqualified him as the Messiah (see Deuteronomy 21:23; Galatians 3:13–14), Jesus wielded power through submission and service and achieved victory through sacrifice and surrender. In this way, he became the once and for all sacrifice that atoned for the sin of humanity (Hebrews 7:26–27). He could die for the sins of humanity because he was one of us, yet he could atone for the sins of humanity because he was not burdened by sin as we are.

THE LAST WILL BE FIRST

On several occasions, Jesus made the comment, "The first will be last, and the last will be first" (for example, see Matthew 19:30). This mysterious statement points to the fact that the values of the world are not the same as the values of God. Therefore, the people whom the world assumes are closest to God and his kingdom might actually be the farthest away. To put it another way, our ways are not God's ways (see Isaiah 55:8). In fact, the values of the world are often the polar opposite of the values of the

kingdom of God. We live as ambassadors in this world, working under the regime of a foreign (sometimes hostile) power, while trying to live up to the expectations and laws of our homeland. But sometimes the values of the kingdom of God seem in conflict with those of the world.

In the Parable of the Laborers in the Vineyard (Matthew 20:1–16), Jesus made the point that God's people don't get what they deserve. But this is good news, because we actually get better than we deserve. We deserve to get justice, but because of Christ, we are offered mercy and reconciliation. God forgives, and then God goes even further and calls us holy. We are holy not because we are perfect, but because we are set apart from the world as God's own. This creates the paradox of the holy sinner. God knows we are not perfect, yet God asks us to strive for a perfection that we will never achieve in this life.

You have probably had the experience of a parent telling you to "act your age." Maybe you have also been that parent. When parents say that, they're not saying, "Act fifteen so that someday you will be fifteen." They're saying, "Act fifteen because you *are* fifteen!" It's the same way with God, your heavenly Father. When God says, "Be holy, for I am holy" (Leviticus 11:44), he's not saying, "Act holy so that someday you will be holy." He's saying, "Act holy, because you *are* holy to me!" Of course God's own holiness includes a perfection that ours does not, but the point is that

God calls us holy because we are his children. This is part of your identity as a child of God. You are loved by the God of the universe. The God of the galaxies is concerned for individuals; he has set you apart as his own and wants a relationship with *you*. And while God recognizes that you are still imperfect, he calls you to rise above your imperfection and aspire to live up to your true potential as a human created in his image.

But God has not created a race of robots. Just as God is a rational being with free will, God has given us the gift of freedom and the rationality to exercise it. In yet another paradox, the people that God created in his own image even have the freedom to reject their Creator. We are free servants of a God who only wants our devotion if it comes by our own free will. This means that some people will make mistakes, and some people will reject God altogether. Even within the Church, some leaders will become distracted by the temptations of pleasure, pride, and power (see Matthew 4:1–11). But that does not excuse us from participation in the Church. We have to resist our own temptation to take a self-righteous attitude and throw the baby out with the bathwater. God is not to blame for the misuse of human free will. Nor is Christianity to blame. Those who would find a rationale for rejecting the Church because of the faults of its leaders are just looking for an excuse to justify spiritual apathy. The truth is, God is continually extending invitations to his people. The invitation is to the forgiveness of the new covenant, to reconciliation with the Creator through his Christ, and to a relationship with God that will endure for eternity. The only unforgivable sin is the rejection of God's offer of forgiveness.

THE KINGDOM OF GOD: IT'S HERE NOW AND IT'S NOT HERE YET

When Jesus came to our world, he preached about the kingdom of heaven, also called the kingdom of God. He said the kingdom was "near" (Matthew 3:2, 4:17, 10:7; Mark 1:15) and is "among you" (Luke 17:21). But the kingdom was not (and still is not) present in its fully revealed state; somehow it is still yet to come (see Matthew, 24:3; Luke 23:42). When Jesus came, he brought the kingdom, but in its hidden form like the mustard seed buried in the ground or the yeast folded into the dough (see Matthew 13:31–33). Yet Jesus promised that what was concealed would someday be revealed (see Luke 12:2, 17:30). At his return, the kingdom will be revealed like the full-grown mustard plant or the risen bread.

In his Parable of the Wedding Banquet (Matthew 22:1–14), Jesus compared the (revealed) kingdom to a wedding reception—a party. Those who were at the party were simply the ones who accepted the invitation. But this parable is as much about the present time, the age of the Church, as it is about the kingdom. When Jesus came two millennia ago, we as the Church became like a bride-to-be, engaged to the Groom (see Mark 2:19). When he returns, he will take us to his home as his bride (see Ephesians 5:25–32; John 14:2–3). The engagement has been announced, and the invitations have gone out, and we who live in the Church age exist in the time between the engagement and the wedding (see Matthew 25:1–13). Another parable that says the same thing but with a different analogy is the Parable of the Weeds Among the Wheat (Matthew 13:24–30, 36–43). In this parable, we live in the time between the planting and the harvest. In the meantime, we wait for the kingdom to be revealed. We have to live with evil in the world, since God allows free will and gives humanity as much time as possible to turn to him and accept him. In fact, we are called to refrain from mental harvesting, judging people as though we know what their eternal destiny will be (Luke 6:36–37). So we try to keep in mind that no one is hopeless, since nothing is impossible for God, and God can redeem anyone.

KOSHER BACON

If our faith is a paradox, then we as believers also become the embodiment of that paradox. We are the *holy sinners* who recognize that we are far from perfect, but God calls us his own anyway. We are the *forgiven guilty*, who try (but

often fail) to live out the values of the kingdom—values which are often backwards in the eyes of the world that tempts us, and yet we get far better than we deserve. We are like *kosher bacon*, a seeming contradiction in terms—we are the unclean made clean. Recognizing this about ourselves should motivate us to treat others with compassion, forgiveness, and patience, since "what God has made clean, you should not call profane" (Acts 10:15).

This is the home for your spirit: living in the paradox of apparent contradictions, embracing the mystery, finding balance in your life by looking for the happy medium between the extremes. We find peace in life by being like Goldilocks, looking for the middle way. Prepare financially for your future, yet not to the extent of postponing all enjoyment in life. Get rid of the things that cause you stress, but allow yourself to enjoy the things that reduce your stress. Respect your body—do not indulge it, but also do not punish it. Be willing to set aside some instant gratification in favor of activities that will make you healthier in the long run. Balance time alone with time spent with others. Don't be selfish, but do not be afraid to speak up for yourself. All of these are examples of living a life in balance—rejecting an "either/or" approach to life in favor of "both/and" in moderation. The healthy balance is in the middle way. The truth is in the middle.

We find hope in life by remembering the big picture—living in the here and now while keeping things in the perspective of eternity. The home for your spirit is found in identifying with Jesus Christ as your Lord and Savior and by being a part of his body the Church. It's found in community, the fellowship of believers who are not scandalized by your insistence on living according to the values of the kingdom, even when that looks like a paradox. The relationship that you have with God through Christ and the relationships that you have with fellow believers will continue throughout eternity. If you have a relationship with God in this life, you can trust that it will continue in the next life. However, those who have no relationship with God in this life should not hope to have one in the next life. It's not really any more complicated than that. God wants everyone to be in his loving presence in the kingdom (2 Peter 3:9). If we accept his invitation, if we accept his offer of forgiveness, we will be forgiven. If we reject that offer, we cannot hope to receive what we have rejected. But for those of us who believe, the hope of eternal life is the big picture that puts everything else in perspective. This is our destiny—eternal life in the kingdom of God.

REACH THE DESTINATION BY FOCUSING ON THE JOURNEY

The three most important questions any person asks in his or her life are the questions of identity, meaning, and destiny. Now we have addressed all three. Your identity is in the fact that you are created in the image of your Creator, and you have an ongoing relationship with him through Jesus Christ. You are a Christian—a child of God, whom he calls holy and beloved. The meaning of life is in your relationships with the people you love and who love you. Your destiny is to live eternally in the presence of God and in reunion with your loved ones in the kingdom of heaven.

However, we can't live in this life by focusing only on the next. We live in this life by focusing on the journey, not the destination. Along the way, we keep the destination in mind so that we can keep things in perspective. But we live one day at a time by engaging in a community of those who share our identity. We build on the relationships with God and each other, in the context of the Church, and this is the home for our spirit.

14

A **Home for Your Spirit**: Where You Pray

WE'VE COME to the fifth and last of the homes, the home for your spirit. Because you are created in the image of God, your life will never be complete without an ongoing connection to your Creator. Therefore, this area of your life is certainly "last, but not least." You don't need to work on this area first, and you don't need to have the home for your spirit built before you work on the other homes, but it helps. You definitely can't leave it out altogether, and if you try you will never be completely fulfilled. Those who say they can live without God are, quite frankly, fooling themselves. Blaise Pascal, the seventeenth century mathematician, said something very insightful: "There is a God-shaped vacuum in the heart of every man which cannot be filled by any created thing, but only by God, the Creator, made known through Jesus." Therefore, just as we remain unfulfilled when our creativity goes unexpressed, even more so do we remain unfulfilled when our spirituality goes unexpressed. Your spirituality is an important part of who you are, and to suppress it, while it might seem like the easy path on a Sunday morning when you don't want to get out of bed, is actually holding you back from being your true self.

THE SPIRITUAL TRIPOD

As I mentioned earlier, there are three ways that our spirituality is expressed, and as you might guess, it's not a choice of one or the other but a balance of all three that is the ideal. The three aspects of spiritual expression are like the three legs of a tripod—without any one of them, the whole thing falls down. The three ways that human spirituality is expressed are *corporate worship, personal devotion, and social responsibility.* Corporate worship means worshipping God in a liturgical service along with an assembly or congregation of fellow believers. The word "corporate" here has nothing to do with the business world; it simply means a group of people acting together. Jesus said, "For where two or three are gathered in my name, I am there among them." (Matthew 18:20). The definition of worship includes both service of and submission to God, and in this context, it means gathered liturgical and traditional rituals that express our desire to submit to God's will and serve him in our lives. When we worship God, we join with others in expressing our gratitude toward God through praise, prayer, and acts of obedience, including the Eucharist (see Luke 22:19). We are taught and encouraged to live according to the values of the kingdom of God, and we encourage each other through mutual support and prayer.

Personal devotion is private time alone with God in contemplation and prayer. This means taking time to connect with God on your own, apart from formal services. Throughout the history of the Church, many contemplatives have experimented with different forms of prayer, including various kinds of meditation, centering prayer, *lectio divina* (prayerfully reading Scripture), prayer beads such as the rosary, and eucharistic adoration. I encourage you to try any or all of these to find what works for you, and what will motivate you to make time for personal devotion. The most important thing is to realize that going to church one hour a week is not enough to connect with your Creator. Think of yourself like the battery in your cell phone. You have to plug it in to recharge the battery on a regular basis or the phone will stop working. Depending on the model of your phone and on how much you use it, sometimes the battery will go longer without needing a charge, and other times it will need to be charged more often.

Prayer is like plugging in to the power source and recharging your spiritual and emotional batteries. We need to be connected to the power of God just to get through life, and especially if you want to live life intentionally and with meaning and fulfillment. And if you try to live on just an hour of recharging per week, that's probably not enough. However, because there are no two of us alike, I can't tell you how often you need to pray. Some people need to pray more often than others. Some weeks we need to pray more than other weeks, depending on what's going on in our lives. But I'm convinced that it is not enough just to go to church and participate in corporate worship. Everyone needs at least some private prayer between church services to stay connected to the divine power Source. Saint Augustine wrote, "You have made us for yourself, O Lord, and our heart is restless until it rests in you." If you want peace in your life, you won't find it without prayer.

Finally, the third way that we express our spirituality is through social responsibility. Like the expression, "pay it forward," we show our love and gratitude to God by loving others in God's name. Social responsibility can take several forms. It can mean works of compassion or charity (see Matthew 25:31–46), it can mean working for justice for those who are helpless or oppressed (see Zechariah 7:9–10), or it can mean evangelization—sharing the good news of Christ and the ministry of reconciliation (see 2 Corinthians 5:17–21). When Jesus was asked about the greatest commandment, he summarized all ten commandments into two: love God and love your neighbor. Then he made sure to clarify that your neighbor is anyone who needs your help (see Luke 10:25–37). These two commandments of Jesus go together. The first leads to the second, and the second flows from the first. There is a priority, in the sense that you have to seek Christ before you can serve him—you cannot give what you have not received (see Luke 10:38–42)—but the gifts of God must be shared, or we disrespect the Giver.

Another way to look at this is to say that there are two aspects to our spiritual life, the vertical and the horizontal. The vertical aspect is our relationship with God, expressed through corporate worship and personal devotion. The horizontal aspect is when we take our relationship with God out into the world. This is expressed in love for neighbor and in evangelization. Like the cross of Christ, the vertical beam points toward heaven, and the horizontal beam causes us to stretch out our arms in love toward others.

THE VERTICAL BEAM: YOUR RELATIONSHIP WITH YOUR CREATOR

We began by defining our identity in terms of our relationship with God. You are a child of God, and that should give you a healthy self-image. But we balance self-esteem with humility, as we try to live in submission to the will of God. In other words, we are not our own highest authority. In fact, there is a certain freedom in letting go of the responsibility of having to be your own god, and there is liberation in submitting to something greater than yourself. That *something* is of course God, but the visible expression of belonging to God is membership in the Church. We belong to something greater than ourselves when we belong to the body of Christ, the Church.

We all need to worship our Creator to be fully human. In fact, we aren't realizing our potential as human beings created in the image of God if we aren't worshipping our Creator. A major part of worship is the acknowledgement of our place in the universe relative to God. He is God, and we're not. We exist to serve him, not the other way around. Therefore, it is wrong to treat God like a cosmic vending machine, as though simply reciting the right prayer or reciting enough prayers will get us what we want. And it is also wrong to come to God in prayer only when you want something. There is nothing wrong with coming to God often in prayer, bringing even the most trivial concerns to him. But we do so admitting that our comfort is not God's first concern. The truth is that as we mature in our spirituality, we are increasingly able to admit that we don't know what's best for us. Only God knows what's best for us in the long run.

Although we are created in the image of God, that image is distorted by our tendency to sin. The image is still there, but it's tarnished. That means we can't always see clearly to make the right decisions (see 1 Corinthians 13:12). Spiritual growth is like cleaning and polishing the image of God within us, so that we are little-by-little restored to a closer likeness to Christ. This is how we work toward realizing our potential as human beings and being at our best. In fact, fulfillment in life is closely connected to being at your best. But remember that this is a process. It is not completed in one moment of conversion or in one mountaintop experience. This is why I continually emphasize focusing on the journey rather than the destination. The destination is heaven, and we won't achieve perfection until we get there. So that should take some of the pressure off. But along the way, we still try to be our best, and we can only do that with support from fellow believers in the Church. The bottom line is, you will never reach your potential (and therefore you will never be truly fulfilled in life) without attending to the spiritual aspect of life. And this can't be done alone. It can only be done in community.

DOING GOD'S WILL

If a person can admit these two things to him or herself—that I am not the center of the universe, and I don't always know what's best for me—then that person can begin to act more and more like Christ, or in other words, more and more according to the will of God. When we think of the will of God in our lives, we often make the mistake of thinking only of the big decisions. But focusing on the journey means paying attention to the little things. God may not give you a sign to show you which decision to make, but God has already given you clear direction on how to do his will. In Paul's letter to the Galatians, he encourages his audience to exhibit certain character traits he calls the "Fruit of the Spirit" (Galatians 5:22–23). The Fruit of the Spirit is the "produce" or the product of the guiding of the Holy Spirit in one's life. It includes love, joy, peace, patience, kindness, generosity, faithfulness, gentleness, and self-control. It is safe to assume that it is always God's will for us to have these traits and to treat others in these ways. If you can learn to think of God's will in terms of these traits, then when the big decisions come along, just ask yourself which course of action will allow you to be a more loving, joyful, peaceful, patient, kind, generous, faithful, gentle, and temperate person.

I should probably say at this point that I don't pretend to be writing this as one who is spiritually superior. To prove my point, I'll tell you one of my big problems. I'm a complainer. I'm quick to complain, automatically muttering my discontent at the slightest inconvenience, whether or not there is anyone there to hear it (of course God hears it). Now let me tell you why this is so wrong. Complaining is arrogant. Complaining comes from the self-righteous assumption that we deserve something better than what we are getting at the time. But the truth is that by God's grace, most of us get far more and better than we deserve most of the time. So complaining is forgetting to be grateful to God and to acknowledge his gifts and blessings. I admit that when I complain about how slow the traffic is going or how long the lines are at the grocery store or whatever it is, I am choosing to focus on the negative, and I am forgetting to count my blessings. I am forgetting that I am not the center of the universe, that God does not exist to serve me, and that in fact, I often don't know what's best for me anyway (maybe slow traffic is saving me from something worse that I'll never know about!). So I invite you to join me in the struggle against complaining and in striving to replace complaining with the one thing that can turn a frustration into a joy: counting our blessings.

DEALING WITH SUFFERING

But what about when there really is something to complain about? What about the times we really do get dealt a hand that is not what we deserve? Being a child of God doesn't shield us from suffering, injustice, or tragedy. How do we respond when we face true suffering or rejection? In reality, every instance of suffering is unique, and every person is unique, so we cannot expect to find a "how to" manual for dealing with suffering. However, there are some overarching principles to keep in mind when facing suffering. The first principle to remember is that God is not responsible for suffering or evil. Evil is not something that God created along with the rest of creation. Evil is in fact the absence (or rejection) of God's goodness, just as darkness is the absence of light, or cold is the absence of heat. Evil and suffering exist in the world because of the misuse of human free will. Even seemingly random tragedies occur because the existence of human free will implies a world where God chooses not to control every variable. This isn't heaven— that comes later. The point is that when you experience suffering or rejection, and you feel like you're left with a hole in your heart—don't blame God for the hole, let God fill the hole. Remember Blaise Pascal and the God-shaped vacuum? When you are suffering, God wants to be there with you. But unfortunately, we all know people who have reacted to suffering by pushing God away. Don't do that—let the suffering push you toward God, not away from him. As we read in Psalm 23, God promises to be with us, even when we walk through the valley of the shadow of death. I once wrote a song based on Psalm 23 that was recorded by my music group, Remember Rome. It's called

"I Will Be With You," and it's written from the perspective as if God is speaking:

Life gives no promises, no guarantees
This isn't heaven, it's not supposed to be
So don't believe them if they tell you
It should be all mountain tops
There are valleys too. . .You know it's true

And the only thing you need to know
When you find yourself in the shadows
I will be with you, I will be with you
I will be with you, I will be there

Life is a long chain of second chances
So don't ever be afraid to learn new dances
And when you find it's time to start again
And you need a trusted hand
To comfort you. . .To walk with you

The only thing you need to know
When you find yourself in the shadows
I will be with you, I will be with you
I will be with you, I will be there

Another principle to remember in times of suffering is that while God will never leave you, and in fact God wants to go through your suffering with you, that does not mean God will rescue you from the suffering. Sometimes the only way to get through something is to go *through* it. Sometimes you can't avoid it. The point is that we have a tendency to look for God to rescue us, and so we're looking for God to make his presence known in some big way. But by looking for God in the big things, we can miss how God reveals his presence in the small things. Then we think God isn't there, or that God has abandoned us. But it's not that God isn't there, it's just that we can't see him because we're looking for him to serve us, rather than asking how we can serve him in this situation. Just as when the Lord came to Elijah (1 Kings 19:11–12), Elijah looked for God in the tornado and in the earthquake and in the fire, but God wasn't in any of these. God was in the whisper of a gentle breeze. How many times do we miss noticing the presence of God in the whisper because we're focusing on the tornadoes and earthquakes? God will come to you in your suffering, but often he will not be what you expect. He may not bring a miraculous rescue, but be open to the presence of God anyway, wherever he may be found, even in the small things of everyday life. Sometimes, being humble means being willing to see God in the small things. The proud demand to be impressed and refuse to acknowledge the presence of God unless he comes in like the cavalry. But the humble people who are willing to see God in the everyday things are generally happier people, because they are quicker to count their blessings, quicker to recognize a gift from God, and more likely to live on gratitude.

Sometimes God is present to us through other people. Therefore, don't allow yourself to go through suffering alone. I know it can be embarrassing, or even painful to let others know what you're going through. However, it will be worse if you try to do it on your own. This is one of the reasons the Church exists, for mutual support and encouragement. Let your brothers and sisters in Christ help you get through your times of suffering. After all, isolating yourself from others during your time of need deprives them of their opportunity to serve God by helping you. Therefore, by shutting others out of your life, you may also be shutting out God.

Finally, when it comes to pain and suffering, be a sponge, not a mirror. This does not mean holding the pain inside or hiding it; it means don't perpetuate it. In other words, don't reflect the pain and spread it around. Instead, absorb it and offer it to God. Remember that it doesn't ease your pain to spread it to others, and it won't make it any more painful if you refuse to inflict pain on others. But you can ease the pain of those around you if you can learn to be a pain sponge. Accept the pain, and dedicate it to the glory of God. And then when someone else is in pain, be with them and share their pain, and absorb it as much as you can. Think about being in a canyon or in a large stone building. If you yell, there will be an echo. The more the walls reflect the sound, the longer it lasts. But if the walls are porous and absorb the sound, it dies out quickly. Suffering is like that echo. The more you can absorb it by accepting it, the faster it will decay. The more you reject it and reflect it, the longer it will last.

SERVANTHOOD

The essence of the Christian life is assuming an attitude like Jesus, "not to be served, but to serve" (Mark 10:45). This means thinking of yourself as a servant of God, and thinking of of others even in the times when it is most tempting to think of yourself first. This is true humility, the desire to serve God and others above yourself. It's not easy, and often it seems to go against the grain of human nature, but experience teaches us that if we don't choose to be humble on our own, we may be humbled or even humiliated by others. Remember Jesus' words about sitting down at the table? It's better to take a seat of lower status and be asked to move up, than to presume to take a seat of higher status and be humbled when someone else says, "You're in my seat" (see Luke 14:7–11).

In our relationship with God, we have to let ourselves be guided, not always having to be in control. You may have seen the bumper sticker that says, "God is my co-pilot," however I think it is more appropriate if *we* take the co-pilot's seat and let God be the pilot. This means that when things don't go our way, we should count our blessings and not complain. This is true even when our prayers seem to go unanswered. It's been said that God always answers prayer, but sometimes the answer is "no." This may seem to trivialize prayer, but there is a grain of truth in it. However, we can only see it as truth if we are willing to admit that God knows what we need better than we do. Remember: humility is being satisfied with what you have but unsatisfied with the way you are. Pride is being satisfied with the way you are but unsatisfied with what you have. And pride always does more harm than good—primarily because it comes between us and our God.

As we have already seen, one aspect of humility and servanthood was especially important to Jesus, and that was forgiveness. In the Parable of the Unforgiving Servant (Matthew 18:23–35), Jesus taught that the refusal to forgive each other is itself a sin. So this is a perfect example of how pride can come between us and God. When we hold a grudge and refuse to forgive someone, we are really only hurting ourselves by driving a wedge between us and God. Lack of forgiveness will short-circuit every other aspect of your spiritual life, so if you think you are holding on to anger toward someone, it would be a good idea to deal with it and get rid of it. I know this can be difficult, because often we feel as though an injustice has been done to us and if we were to forgive too easily, then the other

person would be getting away with something without any consequences. But you are not the judge in this situation. Leave the consequences up to God. In any case, holding a grudge does not punish the other person; it only punishes you by souring your spirituality. Don't wait until you feel ready to forgive. When Jesus said we have to forgive each other from the heart (see Matthew 18:35), he was not talking about an emotion or a warm fuzzy feeling. Remember, in Jesus' time, the heart was not the place of emotions, but the place where decisions come from—the heart was the will. In other words, Jesus was saying that even if you don't feel like forgiving, make a *decision* to forgive. Make this decision based on the knowledge that God has forgiven you for so many things, and turn your gratitude for God's forgiveness into compassion for the person who wronged you. Admit you are no better than that person in many ways. Admit that it takes two to have a conflict and that you may have contributed to escalating the problem to the point of anger. Pray for the person you need to forgive and for God's help in moving on without the anger.

Pride and anger will always come between you and God. But you have a right to a relationship with your Creator, without having to justify it to anyone. Therefore, do not feel that you will be letting anyone down (including yourself) by extending forgiveness to another person or by letting go of anger. You may even be angry at God for something that happened to you or a loved one. But remember God is not the author of evil, and God wants to walk through your suffering with you, if you are willing to look for the ways he is in your life. Think of it in terms of the health of your own spirituality, and don't let anything stand in the way of your access to the Divine. If you look at it this way, letting go of anger can be liberating. Remember, you are not letting anyone down by surrendering the anger and letting God worry about justice. You can't afford to let your feelings of injustice come between you and your Creator, and in any case, you can't handle the responsibility of trying to be your own god. Trying to do that will only prolong the suffering, and you may find you never get past it. Don't waste your mental, emotional, and spiritual energy on anger or holding a grudge. Spend it on getting closer to God. As the apostle James said, "Draw near to God, and he will draw near to you" (James 4:8). Remove the barriers between yourself and God through confession and forgiveness, and invest some time in your prayer life and in worship.

NOT QUANTITY OR QUALITY

When it comes to our faith, it's not the quantity of faith and prayer that matters. In fact, Jesus said that the smallest amount of faith is enough to get started and grow to something great (Luke 17:6). This is why I said that there is no standard

amount of time that everyone should spend in prayer. Some people need more prayer than others. But everyone needs to pray. The truth is that faith is like a muscle. It grows with use and with exercise. The more you stretch your faith, the more it will grow. We stretch our faith by moving beyond the familiar to serve others. Then our past experience of the presence of God in our lives becomes the foundation for ongoing faith in the future. In the Old Testament, the people of Israel were constantly reassuring themselves that God would be with them in the future by reminding themselves of what God did among them in the past. Their past experience with God strengthened their faith in the present and their trust in God for the future. So no matter how much faith you have right now, if you use what you have, it will grow. No amount of faith is too small for God to work with you.

Just as faith and prayer are not a matter of quantity, they are also not a matter of quality. There is no standard of sincerity or depth that you have to measure up to. No one can tell you that your faith is not good enough. It *is* good enough, and it is enough—if your faith is correctly placed. In other words, it is not the quantity or the quality, but the *object* of your faith that matters. Any amount of faith placed in God will grow. No amount of faith, however strong or sincere, will grow if placed in another object. An analogy might be an investment. Any amount of money invested in a sure thing will be rewarded. No amount of money invested in a foolish risk will yield a favorable result.

FAITH AND ICE FISHING

I'm not a cold weather person, but I've witnessed people who enjoy something called ice fishing. They go out in the winter on a frozen lake, cut a hole in the ice, and fish through the hole. Some of them even put up a little shack over the hole, so they can sit out there all day waiting for the fish to bite.

Imagine that two guys want to go ice fishing. Let's call them Barney and Fred. Imagine Barney loads his ice fishing gear into his pickup truck and drives out to the lake. He stops at the edge of the frozen lake and he gets out of the truck. He walks up to the ice and lightly steps on it, gradually putting a little more weight on the ice as he finds that it holds him up. He walks out to the middle of the lake, slowly, listening for any cracking sounds. Then when he gets to the place where he wants to fish, he cuts a hole in the ice and finds that the ice is quite thick—thick enough to hold him, his ice fishing shack, and even his truck. So he drives his truck out onto the ice, sets up his shack, and enjoys a day of ice fishing.

Now imagine that Fred also loads his gear into the back of his pickup truck and drives to the lake. When he gets to the edge of the lake,

the ice looks fine, so without even slowing down, he drives his pickup truck out to the middle of the lake. About a minute after he gets out of the truck, the ice cracks. Before he knows it, his truck, his ice fishing shack, and all his gear are at the bottom of the lake.

So who had more faith, Barney or Fred? Clearly, Fred had more faith. But his faith was misplaced. Although Barney had less faith, he tested his faith and found that his faith was placed in something trustworthy, so his faith grew. God is like the thick ice that will hold you up. It's OK if your faith is tentative at first. God will prove trustworthy and your faith will grow. But if you put your faith in anything other than God, it doesn't matter how strong or how sincere your faith is, it won't hold up. So if anyone tells you that it doesn't matter what you believe, as long as you believe it sincerely, just tell them about Fred and the thin ice.

In actual practice, faith grows in part because it is encouraged by the faith of others. You can imagine that Barney's faith in the ice would have been reassured by seeing others already out on the lake safely fishing. This is why we all need community to be fulfilled in our spirituality— each person's faith strengthens the faith of the others, and everyone's faith grows.

As members of the Church, each of us (hopefully) learns that we are not the center of the universe. The world does not exist to serve us;

in fact, the truth is it's the other way around. Our job is to serve God and neighbor in the world. We can't mature spiritually (which means we can't mature as a whole person in all five areas of life) on our own—we need to be in community with others who will give us a reality check from time to time and to whom we are held accountable. On our own, it's too easy to become self-centered and to justify selfish and unhealthy behavior. But as a member of a faith community, we are constantly reminded of our responsibility to others, not to mention the fact that there are always other people whose problems are worse than our own.

THE HORIZONTAL BEAM:
YOUR RELATIONSHIP WITH YOUR NEIGHBOR

The horizontal aspect of your spirituality is where you are engaged in the world. Saint Basil, the fourth century bishop of Caesarea, once criticized the hermits by saying, "If you always live alone, whose feet will you wash?" What he meant was that if you only focus on worship and prayer, you can't fulfill Jesus' command to love your neighbor. Remember, your spiritual life is like a tripod, and without that third leg of social responsibility, it won't stand. In reality, there is no way we could ever repay God for all his blessings, not least of which is forgiveness and salvation. We can't repay him, because there is nothing he needs. So the way we show our gratitude to God is by serving our neighbor.

To be a child of God is to be both called and sent. We are called into a relationship with God through Christ, and from that relationship, we are sent out to serve others in the name of Christ. We are called to worship and prayer (including prayerful study of the Scriptures), and what we receive from our worship, prayer, and study we are expected to share with others. As I've said before, the gifts of God are not meant to be kept to ourselves; they are meant to be given away. But without regular corporate worship and prayer, we have nothing to give when we try to serve others. We all need first to connect to the power Source, and then take that power into the world. By virtue of our baptism, we are all ministers of the Gospel. We may not all be clergy, but we are all ministers. Therefore, we are sent out to do ministry: works of mercy, charity, and compassion, as well as evangelization. We are sent into the world to live the life to which we've been called and to follow the example set by Christ. Then we invite those we encounter to come back with us and experience the community of the Church. The whole thing becomes a cycle in which the sheep become shepherds and more sheep are added to the flock.

We have already explored the connection between mind and body, and now we see that there is also a connection between spirit and body. It is through our bodies that we are active in the world, and as spiritual creatures, we are expected to be concerned for the bodily well-being of others. It is not ministry to offer someone the good news of the Gospel but leave them hungry (see Matthew 25:31–46). Of course it also does no good to feed the hungry if they don't know why you're doing it (see Matthew 5:16). The early Christians believed that "the bellies of the poor are the storehouses of God." In other words, if you want to store your treasures in heaven (see Matthew 6:19–21), make an investment in feeding the hungry.

THE GOSPEL ACCORDING TO STEVE

More than one generation is familiar with the song, "Fly Like an Eagle" by Steve Miller. In what I like to call "The Gospel According to Steve," we hear these words: "Feed the babies who don't have enough to eat/shoe the children with no shoes on their feet/house the people living in the street." I would say that's a pretty good summary of some of Jesus' own teaching (for example, Matthew 25:37–40). When you read the Gospels, you will find that one word more than any other describes Jesus' motivation in ministering to people. That word is *compassion*. Jesus had compassion for people—he loved them and wanted to help them. Most of all, he wanted them to know the love and presence of God in their lives. This led him to talk to those whom the proud would ignore, minister to those whom the self-righteous would condemn, and touch those whom no one else

would even look at. His favorite context for ministry seems to have been mealtime. He sat down at the table and ate with them and talked to them and encouraged them and reassured them that God had not forgotten them. He told them it was never too late to accept the invitation of God.

For what groups or types of people do you feel compassion? Who are you concerned about? Whom do you want to help? What would it mean for you to go out of your way to sit down and eat with them? This can be a scary thought. Certainly it's probable that going out of your way like Jesus did might be uncomfortable. But this is what we mean when we say faith is like a muscle, and it grows by being stretched. The point is to give away what we have been given: compassion, forgiveness, and reconciliation with God—to pass along the good news of God's offer of forgiveness and invitation to salvation. We didn't deserve the grace we were given, so why should we wait until others deserve it before we pass it on? Saint Francis of Assisi reminded people that we are all beggars compared to God. Therefore our life and works should be motivated by gratitude for the great gifts God has given us in Christ.

BEING GOLDILOCKS

Being Goldilocks in the realm of spirituality means finding a balance of devotion and service. A spirituality that is all devotion and no service is self-centered and ignores the second of the two greatest Commandments. The Apostle James said that works are the evidence of faith, and if you have no good works, it calls your faith into question (see James 2:14–26). On the other hand, a spirituality that is all service and no devotion is equally empty—it is attempting to give something you don't have. In truth there is a logical priority in which you first must receive the gifts from Jesus before you can pass them on. The story of Martha and Mary (Luke 10:38–42) shows that you have to seek Christ before you can serve him. But to receive the gifts and keep them to yourself would be to stop with the job half done. We cannot reduce this to an argument of faith versus works. In fact, such a dichotomy is quite artificial (see John 6:29). The Apostle Paul wrote that we are not saved by works, but then was quick to add that we *are* created to do good works (Ephesians 2:8–10). Therefore, the Christian faith (and human potential) can only be fully expressed in the context of a church community. Without that community, an important part of your spirituality (and an important part of who you are) would be stifled and suppressed.

Everyone needs to belong. This is also another aspect of the home for your heart, which demonstrates again the overlap between the five homes. You've probably heard the expression that there is no "I" in "team." In the same way, there is no "my" in the Our Father. Notice how the prayer that Jesus taught his disciples is meant to be prayed by a group, not by individuals alone. That tells you something important. We need each other, and we are the body of Christ, not individually but collectively. We find our identity in our relationship with God, but we cannot be in relationship with God apart from the Church. We identify with Christ, and by calling him our Lord, Savior, and brother, we become children of God (John 1:12–13). However, the primary way that we identify with Christ is in baptism, where we symbolically die and rise with Christ in the sacramental water. After baptism, we continually identify with Christ in many ways, from sticking a fish symbol on our cars to saying the historic creeds of the Church to crossing ourselves. All these are ways of identifying ourselves as people who belong to Christ, the most important of which is participation in the Eucharist. But it all implies not only membership in Christ, but membership in his Church.

WHAT DO WE MEAN WHEN WE SAY "THE CHURCH"?

No matter what denomination we belong to, we are all part of the one worldwide body of Christ (1 Corinthians 12:27). The communion of saints is a unity in the Holy Spirit of all Christians in all times and places (Hebrews 12:1). It is worldwide, and it includes the past, present, and future, connecting us in Christ to our brothers and sisters across the world and across the span of history. We are connected to each other and to our fellow Christians on the other side of the earth, and also to those who have gone before us and are now in heaven. This is how you belong to something bigger than yourself. In fact, it is not only bigger than yourself, it is bigger than everything else except for God. The Church goes way beyond your local congregation. The communion of saints spiritually connects us to the Christians of the past, to all Christians in the present, and also to the future realm of God when we will all be together in the presence of Christ (Mark 14:25). At that time, we will be unified in a way that is not yet possible due to separations of time, space, and denominational division. But in the meantime, we share a common baptism and a common tradition.

The Tradition of the Church of course includes our Scriptures. We are Christians, and Christians believe that truth comes from revelation, not intuition. In other words, left on our own, we would never come to understand God and his will for us. We need God to reveal himself to us. No amount of contemplation would ever be enough without divine revelation. There is no way that we could reach God by our own effort, but the good news is that in Jesus Christ, God reached out to us. But revelation is not the property of individuals (2 Peter 1:20). Revelation comes to the people collectively, and

the interpretation and translation of God's Word is done in the community. This is the community in which we find our identity as followers of Christ and children of God, and this is why it is virtually impossible to know God apart from community.

Therefore, if you don't have a local church to belong to, get one! You will never have a home for your spirit until you have a church home. It is important to attend worship services regularly. I would like to say weekly attendance is the bare minimum, but I don't want to be legalistic about it, especially if you are not currently attending a church and you need to ease into it. Feel free to shop around and visit several churches before making a commitment to one; however, beware of treating the Church with a consumer mentality. The Church is not a commodity, and you need it more than it needs you! It is understandable to want to attend a church where you like the preacher and the worship style; however, keep in mind that the point is not what you want, but what you need. It is probably more important to belong to a church in your neighborhood so that it becomes part of your local community, rather than traveling a distance to find the "perfect" church (hint: there's no such thing). In fact, if you have to travel more than ten to fifteen minutes to get to worship, it becomes too easy not to go, especially when you're running late on a Sunday morning.

Beyond weekly worship, work your way up to some involvement during the week and involvement in some ministry to help the less fortunate. This will help you put your own life in perspective, reminding you to count your blessings and encouraging you to live your life out of gratitude. If you can get to the point where you attend weekly worship and engage in some prayer or Bible study during the week and participate in some ministry to others, you will have the three aspects of your spirituality covered: worship, devotion, and service. Of course, devotion can be done privately at home, but the other two cannot. This is why belonging to a church community is essential for fully expressing your spirituality.

WHY DO I NEED ORGANIZED RELIGION? CAN'T I JUST BE SPIRITUAL?

It should be apparent by now that personal devotion is only one leg of the tripod that is the home for your spirit. Without belonging to a faith community, you simply can't live a fulfilled life. I know there are people who think that their lives are complete without a connection to a church, but to put it simply, they just don't know what they're missing. We all need encouragement from a group that accepts us unconditionally. And without that encouragement, we cannot live up to our potential. But in addition to encouragement, we also need accountability. In other words, we need people who will give us the occasional reality check and call us out when we start to live in denial about our own faults. Usually this happens in a general way when we listen to the preacher interpret the Scriptures. But sometimes we need actual confrontation to make us wake up and realize we've strayed off the path. Hopefully, a church will have a few people who will tell us the truth even when it's not what we want to hear. In my experience, the truth really will set you free (see John 8:32), even when you're afraid to hear it. On the other hand, deception is contagious, and while we may not think of ourselves as deceptive people, it's too easy to lie to yourself when you're trying to express your spirituality on your own.

The most common way that people lie to themselves is by convincing themselves that the path of least resistance is the way they are called to go. They choose the course of action (or inaction) that requires the lowest level of commitment and allows the highest level of comfort. But if you've ever talked to someone who left comfort behind to go on a mission trip, they will most likely tell you that it was worth it. All this is to say that you can't be a church of one. It just doesn't work. Of course people have been trying to do it almost since the beginning of Christianity. They take the parts of the faith they like and set aside the parts that seem too demanding or that don't fit with their image of what they think God should be like. The theological term for this is *syncretism*, but it could be called the "salad bar" approach to spirituality. It amounts to picking and choosing only those aspects of the faith you like, combining them with aspects of other religions that sound appealing, and ultimately creating your own personal religion. But isn't that the sin of Adam and Eve? They presumed to determine for themselves what is right and wrong, true and false, which amounted to the attempt to make themselves their own highest authority. When you take it upon yourself to discard whatever parts of the faith don't appeal to you, aren't you making yourself your own god? But our faith is not man-made. It goes back through an unbroken chain to the Apostles and to Jesus himself. Ultimately our religion comes, not from human reason, but from God's revelation. On your own, you may try to reach up to God, but it can't be done. However, God has reached down to us in Jesus Christ and has opened up access to him through his Church. Therefore, by belonging to *a church*, you belong to *the Church*, the body of Christ, and you are part of something vastly more important and more timeless than anything humanity could ever create.

BUT I DON'T GET ANYTHING OUT OF GOING TO CHURCH!

Who said you were supposed to get anything out of it? This is not about you, and it's not about what you *get*. It's all about expressing your spirituality through *giving*. That giving begins with giving thanks to God for his gifts and blessings. In fact, we begin and end with gratitude. Unfortunately, our culture has become increasingly oriented toward entertainment, and we have created a sense of entitlement in people that demands to be served and entertained. Some churches have apparently decided "if you can't beat 'em, join 'em," so they have created worship experiences that cater to the lowest common denominator of people's desire for entertainment. But worship is not meant to be worshipper-centered. It is supposed to be Christ-centered.

The church is where you give back, both vertically and horizontally. Giving back vertically means worshipping God in gratitude. In fact, the word *Eucharist* means "thanksgiving." Giving back horizontally means expressing our gratitude and love for God by loving our neighbor. Remember, the gifts and love of God can only be kept by giving them away. In fact, failure to give away the gifts of God is almost the same as refusing them. When we can learn to approach church membership and worship as a form of giving, only then will we begin to get something out of it. You've heard the expression, "You get out of it what you put into it." That is never more true than when it comes to participation in the Church. If you find yourself looking for a new church, think about whether a particular church is a place where you can *give* rather than *get*. Or at least think about whether you will get what you *need* instead of having to get everything you *want*.

BUT THE CHURCH IS FULL OF HYPOCRITES!

You may expect me to respond by saying, "No, the Church isn't full of hypocrites!" But I can't do that. Those who say that the Church is full of hypocrites are absolutely right. You would be just as right if you said the hospital is full of sick people. But that's exactly where they should be. The Church is not a country club for the perfect people (are there any?). The Church is a hospital for the soul. The real hypocrites are the ones who aren't in church, because they think they don't need religion, or they think they're too good for that crowd. It is true that the Church attracts broken people. But who among us is not broken in some way? That's why we need a Savior. Sure, the Church is full of hypocrites who don't always practice what they preach. In fact, I'm one of them. I wish I could say I always practice what I preach (or write), but that would be a lie. It would be easy enough to make the Church perfect—just kick out all the imperfect people. But who would be left? Not me. This is what I was trying to express when I wrote the song, "Broken Machine":

*Never a day goes by that
I don't say something that
makes me look like a fool
Never a day goes by that
I don't say something that
pushes me farther away from you*

*'Cause I am a broken machine
I am a broken machine
I've got something loose inside
That doesn't let me function right
I am a broken machine
But I hope that you'll remember me
The way that I was meant to be*

*Anything gives me joy
I usually destroy it
You always love the ones you hurt
It's only by grace that I can
Look in your face and hope that
You can see through all the dirt*

'Cause I am a broken machine. . .

Someone once said, "My church is like Noah's Ark: if not for the storm outside, I wouldn't be able to stand the smell inside!" I think that illustrates the point that no local church is perfect, and no denomination is perfect. But is that an excuse to avoid belonging? If you leave church membership out of your life just because there are imperfect people there, you miss the opportunity that you and those other imperfect people might just help each other improve toward realizing your potential as human beings. Whether or not they can do it without you, you can't do it without them.

Finally, if you leave church membership out of your life, you also miss out on significant opportunities for encounter with God. And isn't that what spirituality is all about? We long for genuine encounter with the Divine. The other day I was thirsty, so I read a book about water. Guess what? I was still thirsty. Then I was hungry, so I looked at some pictures of food. Guess what? I was still hungry. Reading about spirituality (even this book!) does not replace real encounter with God. Of course you can encounter God in private prayer, but that is only one aspect of spirituality. There are two other aspects: encountering God in worship and encountering God in the people you can help.

THE INVITATION

I want to conclude this chapter with an invitation. When Jesus was asked about the kingdom of heaven, he described it as a wedding banquet (see Matthew 22:1–14). In this parable, invitations eventually went out to everyone. But those who refused the invitation, who made excuses and asked to be excused, missed out on the party. At other times Jesus said, "Whoever welcomes me welcomes the one who sent me" (Mark 9:37; Luke 9:48), and "Everyone therefore who acknowledges me before others, I also will acknowledge before my Father in heaven; but whoever denies me before others, I also will deny before my Father in heaven" (Matthew 10:32–33). Therefore, Jesus presents us with an invitation, but one that requires a response. We are all invited to receive reconciliation with God and an ongoing relationship with God through the forgiveness that Jesus Christ offers. But for this gift to be received, it has to be accepted.

You may be familiar with images of the crucifixion that have a sign on the cross over Christ's head. The sign carries the initials, INRI, short for the Latin words *Iesus Nazarenus, Rex Iudaeorum*, which means "Jesus the Nazarene, King of the Jews" (John 19:19–22). I suggest it would be just as appropriate to imagine the cross with a different set of four letters: RSVP. The cross of Christ stands as an open invitation to a relationship with God and to the realization of a more fully expressed spiritual side to your life. The invitation has been sent. Now God waits for your RSVP. Please respond.

15

Reflection on the **Home for Your Spirit**

THE VERTICAL BEAM

What does it mean to you that your identity is defined by your identification with Christ?

_____

_____

What does it mean to you to be a child of God and brother or sister of Christ?

_____

_____

What does it mean to you that your destiny is to live for eternity in the presence of God?

_____

_____

How does keeping this destiny in mind allow you to see a bigger picture and keep other things in perspective? _____

_____

Think about a conversion experience or an "Ah-ha!" moment that you had. What do you remember as significant about it? How did it change you? _____

_____

How is conversion or sanctification (growth in spiritual maturity) an ongoing experience for you?

_____

What does it mean to you that God is constantly sending invitations and offering a clean slate?

_____

_____

Read Luke 17:11–19. When have you been like the nine lepers who didn't thank Jesus? _____

_____

When have you been like the one leper who went back to thank Jesus? _____

_____

How often do you complain about little things? _____

How often do you count your blessings? _____

What would it mean for you to be more motivated by gratitude? _____

_____

*Consider trying the ecumenical **Gratitude Rosary** at the end of this book to help you count your blessings.*

How often do you pray (outside of church)? _____

Do you only pray when things aren't going well? _____

Do you think you pray enough?_____

If not, what would it be like if you prayed more often? _____

_____

What steps would you have to take to plan to pray more often?_____

_____

_____

THE HORIZONTAL BEAM

What does it mean to you that the meaning of life is found in relationships? _____

_____

What does it mean to you that you are a brother or sister to all children of God? _____

_____

What does it mean to you that your neighbor is anyone who needs your help? _____

_____

Do you have a church you belong to? _____

How often do you attend worship? Is it enough? _____

When you miss weekly worship, what are your reasons for missing? _____

What does it mean to you to be part of the body of Christ and the communion of saints? _____

_____

How does the recognition of your own imperfection and your own ongoing need for conversion or

sanctification give you perspective when dealing with others? _____

What are some of the things God has forgiven you for? _____

What are some of the things others have forgiven you for? _____

Do you see the same kinds of imperfections in other people that God and others have forgiven

in you? _____

Is there something you're holding on to that's hard to forgive? _____

Are you angry at God? _____

Are you holding a grudge or having trouble letting go of anger toward someone? _____

Ask yourself these questions, and answer them honestly:

When have you done the same thing to someone else? _____

What have you done that's even worse? _____

How did you contribute to the problem or escalate the tension? _____

What pain or struggle might the other person be experiencing? _____

If you were to pray for the person you're angry with, what would you pray for? _____

Now say a prayer of thanksgiving to God for all the forgiveness you have received. If you can, pray for the person you are angry with and ask God to help you forgive. Make a decision to forgive, but realize that it's OK if you need to make that decision again tomorrow and the next day. It will take time to feel forgiving.

Read the Parable of the Good Samaritan in Luke 10:30–37. When have you been like the ones who

passed by on the other side of the road? _____

How did you feel afterward? _____

When have you been like the Samaritan and gone out of your way to help someone?_____

_____

How did you feel afterward? _____

BEING GOLDILOCKS

What would it look like to balance devotion and service in your life? _____

How close are you to finding that balance? _____

Evaluation

Which do you think applies to you? Circle all the statements that sound like your situation right now. Then choose one of the categories below:

Rebuild: You have no local church or faith community to belong to. You have little or no prayer life, or you pray only in times of crisis. You feel cut off from the body of Christ and/or the communion of saints, and possibly you feel a distance between you and God. Basically, your tripod has no legs.

Remodel: You belong to a church, but attendance is sporadic and there is little or no involvement beyond weekly worship. You are not involved in ministry to others apart from the occasional donation. You pray, but you feel like your prayers are inadequate, or you wonder if God really hears your prayers, or if in fact there is any point to prayer. Maybe you have one leg of the tripod, but you lack the other two.

Redecorate: You are a member of a church and attend regularly. You have minimal involvement beyond weekly services, and you may be unfamiliar with the Scriptures. Maybe you are involved in ministry, but you lack the foundation of a devotional life to support your good works. Maybe you have an active prayer life, but you have not become involved in ministry. Your tripod has two legs, but you are still missing something.

Appreciate: You have a good home for your spirit. Your tripod has all three legs. You're not perfect, and there is always room for improvement, but you can be thankful for this area of life. Say a prayer of thanksgiving to God for your church community and for the home for your spirit.

16

Rhythm, Not Routine

SOMETIMES WE FEEL as though we're stuck in a rut. We come to resent the routine of our lives because we sense that something is missing. We feel (or we hope) that there must be more to life than what we are experiencing. Whenever I have felt this way in my life, I have been reminded of the very poignant Jackson Browne song, "The Pretender":

I'm going to rent myself a house
in the shade of the freeway
I'm going to pack my lunch in the morning,
and go to work each day
And when the evening rolls around,
I'll go on home and lay my body down
And when the morning light comes
streaming in, I'll get up and do it again
Amen
Say it again. . . Amen

I want to know what became of the changes
we waited for love to bring
Were they only the fitful dreams
of some greater awakening
I've been aware of the time going by,
they say in the end it's the wink of an eye

And when the morning light comes
streaming in, you'll get up and do it again
Amen

Have you ever felt that way? Maybe you feel that way now, and that's why you're reading this book. When I was in a fraternity in college, we had to be able to say the Greek alphabet three times before a match burned down to our fingers. Somehow, at the time, it seemed like a reasonable test of commitment. In any case, the trick was to start with as much air in your lungs as possible, so you wouldn't have to waste time by stopping to breathe. Sometimes life feels like that. Sometimes we get to the point where we have over-scheduled and over-committed ourselves so that we find ourselves beginning a day just wishing it would be over already. We take a deep breath, maybe say a prayer that God will just get us through this day, and we dive in with our eyes closed. When the day is over, we haven't really thought about what we were doing while we were doing it; we were just going through the motions. And then we end the day glad that it's over. But the next day, we *get up and do it again.*

People who come to a point in their lives where they feel like they're in a rut generally have one of two responses. Either they fear change and do nothing but live with the discontent until it turns into frustration or depression, or they opt for radical change—sometimes by creating conflict—and end up exchanging routine for chaos (sometimes we call this a midlife crisis). This latter choice can even take the form of self-destructive escapist behavior, such as substance abuse. However, by now it won't surprise you to find out that I am going suggest a middle way. On the one hand, there is no need to fear change as long as you can be intentional about what you keep and what you let go of. On the other hand, there is no need to exchange the extreme structure of routine for it's polar opposite, lack of structure and chaos. The middle way is to live a life that is characterized by rhythm, not routine.

YOU CAN'T SING A WHOLE SONG IN ONE BREATH

Have you ever tried to sing a whole song in one breath? It can't be done, and even if it could (like the Greek alphabet), it wouldn't be musical. Music is the interplay of sounds and silence, playing and resting. A good song does not consist of constant singing; it has pauses to give the singer time to breathe and the listener time to think. To sing a song and make it sound musical, you sing a phrase and you take a breath. So why do we try to live through a week, or even a day, without taking a breath? We all need to punctuate our days, our weeks, and even our years with a pause to rest and take a spiritual, mental, and emotional breath. It is no coincidence that in both biblical languages of Hebrew and Greek, the word for spirit (including the Holy Spirit) is the same root word that is used to describe wind and breath. This is the breath of life, and without it, our souls will suffocate.

STEPPING STONES

Throughout this book, I've been repeating a theme, specifically that one of the keys to happiness is to look at life as a journey, focus on the journey, and enjoy the journey, rather than see life as goal-oriented or the achieving of some end. In the 1993 film, *Groundhog Day*, starring Bill Murray, a weather man with the same name as the groundhog is doomed to repeat one day over and over again, until he learns the lesson that happiness is found by living in the present. In fact, this movie is an excellent illustration of the concept that life is a journey and is meant to be lived as such.

One way to apply this is to imagine your life as a path made up of stepping stones. If you've ever had to cross a stream by stepping on rocks, you know that they don't present a straight and level path. Therefore, you can't run across stepping stones; you have to take each stone

one at a time and stop on each one to get your bearings for the next step. If you try to take them too fast, or if you look too far ahead, you will fall. Your life is like those stepping stones, and the rhythm of life is in taking the stones one at a time and pausing at each one to be intentional about taking the next step.

Thinking of life as a series of stepping stones also helps when it comes to following Jesus' example and God's plan for our lives. God usually reveals his plan for us as stepping stones, one step at a time, not as a long-term goal. In fact, other than our destiny to spend eternity with God, it is debatable whether there is a long-term goal for everyone. The point is that God shows us the way through life one stepping stone at a time. Each step on the path is an invitation to accept or reject God's leading. The choice we make will determine the next step. But even when we make the wrong choices, there are new invitations and new choices offered, and God can always bring order out of chaos and make some good come out of our wrong turns (see Romans 8:28; Genesis 28:15). As the song, "I Will Be With You" says: "Life is a long chain of second chances."

God will always take the initiative to place new invitations in your path every day. The good news is that you don't need to worry about where the path will ultimately lead, except that you can have confidence that if you commit to the journey, it will eventually lead to the kingdom of heaven. But if you can leave the destination up to God and focus on the journey, and if you can take each step one at a time, you will begin to be more aware of the daily invitations and interventions that come from God. Every day there are new gifts from God, but if we are too quick to get through the day and get it over with, we will miss these times that God reveals himself in our lives. Often God's grace comes to us through our spouses or our brothers and sisters in Christ. This is how God's love and forgiveness comes to us and how God's presence is realized in the everyday events and details of our lives. This grace from God empowers us to become increasingly better at recognizing God's presence and God's gifts and also to use the gifts we have been given to serve others and to be the presence of God in their lives.

JESUS MEETS US WHERE WE ARE AND WALKS WITH US

The same Jesus Christ who walked on water wants to walk with you on the path of your life. But too often we are so focused on looking ahead that we can be like the disciples on the road to Emmaus who didn't recognize the one who was walking with them (see Luke 24:13–36). Wherever you are in your journey, and no matter where you have been or how far off the path you have strayed in the past, Christ is willing to meet you where you are and walk with you from now on. He does not condemn you (see John 8:11). He wants to walk with you and help you along the way. If you think of your life as a series of stepping stones, each day becomes a new opportunity to accept God's invitations, regardless of the past. There is nothing you have done that could make God rescind his invitation. However, recognizing God's gifts and invitations and being intentional about accepting those gifts and invitations requires that we don't try to run across the stones. We have to take them one at a time, pausing regularly to take a breath. These regular pauses become the rhythms of life that allow us to live intentionally and not just let life go by.

We are already familiar with some forms of rhythm. For example, the calendar is punctuated with holidays, some of which mark the passing of seasons or commemorate important events in the past. Many people take a vacation once a year. They stop work for a week or two and do something fun and relaxing. As Christians, we pause once within each week for corporate worship and at certain times each year for the celebration of important events in the life of Christ. Many Christians set aside time for personal prayer and Bible study as often as once a day, or more. The point here is to think about what kinds of rhythm are right for you. What kinds of rhythm will give you time to pause and breathe so that you can live more intentionally,

but without causing a burden or becoming a routine? Remember, these are not frivolous distractions that can be left out of your lifestyle without consequences, but on the other hand, it is not healthy to turn spirituality into a legalistic burden, either. We don't want to trade one kind of routine for another.

Prayer and meditation are known to decrease stress and other health problems, and taking the time for prayerful contemplation will help you make your choices intentionally, instead of letting life's choices get made for you by your circumstances. Play and relaxation will keep you healthy and allow you to live longer. God created order and rhythm out of chaos, and therefore what we want is a holy rhythm that will free up our own creativity without casting us back into chaos. In other words, somewhere between the extremes of routine and chaos is the happy medium of rhythm.

One more thing should be mentioned at this point. There are many religious traditions that have recognized the importance of prayer, meditation, and contemplation. However, some advocate emptying the mind as a way to clarity. I would argue that this is not the Christian way. God created everything out of nothingness. We should not try to get back to the nothingness. The truth is that human nature being what it is, if you try to empty your mind, your subconscious will just fill it with temptations (see Luke

11:24–26). Instead, when we meditate, we should be thinking about God or about something that God would want us to focus on. For example, in Philippians 4:6–8, the Apostle Paul wrote:

Do not worry about anything, but in everything by prayer and supplication with thanksgiving let your requests be made known to God. And the peace of God, which surpasses all understanding, will guard your hearts and your minds in Christ Jesus. Finally, beloved, whatever is true, whatever is honourable, whatever is just, whatever is pure, whatever is pleasing, whatever is commendable, if there is any excellence and if there is anything worthy of praise, think about these things.

If you are new to the idea of contemplative prayer, try the Guided Devotional Experience or the ecumenical Gratitude Rosary at the end of this book. It will help you focus your thoughts and make your prayer a dynamic dialogue with God. These can be repeated with variations so that your prayer is different every time. Just make sure some form of thanksgiving is always a part of your prayers. Whether you use the Guided Devotional Experience, prayer beads, traditional prayers, or just talk to God from your heart, you will find that a regular rhythm of prayer and contemplation will allow you to stop and count

your blessings and then make more intentional choices in life. In addition to daily or weekly prayer, consider a monthly prayer service or annual retreat experience. These will allow you to periodically take stock of your life and evaluate your progress in the journey.

TIME MANAGEMENT

It could be objected at this point that if one's life is chaotic, that probably means there is no time for additional commitments such as worship and prayer or joining social groups or taking classes. I certainly understand that the very problem we began with, that we are over-committed, seems to prevent bringing anything new into our lives. However, this simply means that something has to go. One of the desired effects of the five homes methodology is that life will be simplified so that it's not just about adding the things that are missing, but that it requires first getting rid of the things that cause stress in order to make room for the things that are truly important: time with loved ones and friends, time to relax, and time to exercise. Sacrifices will have to be made. When you are working on the home for your hands, consider working fewer hours. Make sure you have healthy boundaries about working overtime and weekends. Or look for a job that will allow you to work less and have a healthier lifestyle. Maybe you will have to get rid of the car with the big monthly payments in order to work less and enjoy life more. Maybe you will have to downsize your home in order to spend more time with the people who live there. If working fewer hours is not an option for you, some other changes will have to be made. When you are working on the homes for your mind and heart, you may have to back out of some other commitments in order to join that group or take that class. If part of your responsibilities include driving the kids around to several activities a day, you may need to organize car pool shifts with other parents so you have to do it less often, or perhaps even consider whether your children are doing too much. When you are working on the home for your spirit, you may have to miss some weekend activities (including your kids' activities) to get to church. However, do resist the temptation to make more time by getting less sleep, or you will work against your own efforts in building a healthy home for your body. The bottom line is that something has to go

in order to simplify your life and still make time to build all five homes.

Time management doesn't mean being hyper-organized so that you can cram everything into your life with no space between commitments, ultimately sacrificing sleep to get it all done. That is just being a slave to the hamster wheel. Time management means learning how to say no to some people and some opportunities so that you can say yes to God, to your loved ones and friends, and to yourself. Only you can make those choices, but if you can work toward incorporating rhythms that allow you to stop and breathe and make clear-headed decisions (rather than just going along with your circumstances), you will live intentionally by making conscious, self-aware choices. The more you can order your life toward rhythm and not routine, the more you will feel that your lifestyle brings you peace and happiness.

17

Reflection: Putting it All Together

NOW WE HAVE COME to the point where you can begin to evaluate the overall state of your five homes. This chapter will walk you through the steps toward an action plan, and the next chapter will help you outline that plan.

In the space below, list any of your homes that you evaluated as being in the "Appreciate" category. If there are none, that's OK—just leave the space blank.

_____

_____

In the space below, list any of your homes that you evaluated as being in the "Redecorate" category:

_____

_____

In the space below, list any of your homes that you evaluated as being in the "Remodel" category:

_____

_____

In the space below, list any of your homes that you evaluated as being in the "Rebuild" category:

_____

_____

_____

If you have any homes in the Appreciate category, stop now and say a prayer of thanks to God for the way he has blessed you in the related area(s) of your life. The next time you go to church, you might plan to go a few minutes early so you can begin with some quiet time for thanksgiving. Or if your church has a chapel open outside of service times, you may want to stop by there some time this week for a few minutes of thanksgiving prayer in the house of God. After some appropriate thanksgiving, any homes in the Appreciate category will be set aside for the time being as not needing any significant work. Keep doing what you're doing in those areas, and if after working on the other homes you want to come back to them, you certainly can. While you are working on the other homes, be encouraged by whatever you already have built.

Our method will be to start with the homes that are closest to the Appreciate category. In other words, you will begin with any homes that you listed as needing to be redecorated. If there is more than one home in the Redecorate category, start with the easiest. Take a moment to decide which of the homes in the Redecorate category are closest to the Appreciate category. Put a number by each of the homes in the Redecorate category, listing them in order from easiest (closest to Appreciate) to hardest (closest to Remodel). This is the order you will work on them. The objective is to work on each home until you can move it into the Appreciate category, and then move on to work on the next home. Once you have given an order to any homes in the Redecorate category (if there are more than one), then do the same thing with the Remodel category and finally the Rebuild category. In the space below, list all of the homes that were not in the Appreciate category, in order from those that need the least work to those that need the most work. If there is one that you are particularly uncomfortable with, feel free to move it down on the list so that you can put off working on it until later. There is nothing wrong with that, as long as you get started on something. Number your homes starting with one (1) as the first one you will work on.

This is the order in which you will work on your five homes. As each home moves into the Appreciate category, you will give thanks for that and for all the homes in that category, and then you will move on to the next home. The only exception to this is in the home for your heart. If part of what you are looking for in the home for your heart is to find a significant other, I suggest you work on that home last. Or if you prefer, work on the home for your heart in order, but focus on friendships and postpone the search for a significant other until all your other homes have moved into the Appreciate category. This will ensure that your life is in order, making you more attractive to a potential mate.

WHO IS YOUR HERO?

As you think about the areas of your life that need work, is there someone you know who seems to have it together or who is closer to having all the areas of his or her life in order?_____

_____

Why do you think this person has his or her homes in order? _____

_____

_____

In what ways would you hope to be more like this person? _____

_____

_____

Could this person be a mentor to you? _____

Would this person be willing to talk with you periodically as you go through the process of building your five homes?_____

If not, is there someone else who would? _____

_____

If you don't already have a mentor or spiritual director, consider getting one. This might be a professional relationship with someone whom you would pay for his or her services. Or this could simply be a friend who would be willing to have lunch with you once a month or so to talk about your progress. In any case, it would be helpful to have someone to encourage you and keep you focused on the task. List some people whom you might ask to do this for you. Make a plan to choose one and ask him or her if this would be a possibility.

_____

_____

_____

PRIORITIES

Now that you've read through most of this book, think about the following questions:

What is most important to you in your life? _____

_____

Who is most important to you in your life? _____

What is missing from your life *that you feel you can't live without*? (When you can honestly say the answer is "nothing," then it's time to thank God again!) _____

_____

What does the concept of vocation mean to you? _____

_____

What does the concept of career mean to you? _____

_____

What does the concept of retirement mean to you? _____

PASSIONS

Assuming that everyone is creative in some way, how do you express your creativity?_____

_____

What do you want to create or produce that would contribute something to the world, your commu-

nity, or your family, or that would add some beauty to your life? _____

Whom do you want to help, and in what way? _____

_____

Is there some experience you have had that you want to help others have? _____

_____

Is there some experience you have had that you want to help others avoid or endure? _____

_____

PASTTIMES

What is fun to you? _____

What is relaxing to you? _____

How will you incorporate into your life a rhythm of fun and relaxation that will punctuate the times of

work and allow you to pause and breathe? _____

How will you incorporate into your life a rhythm of worship, prayer, and service that will keep your life

in perspective and allow you to express your gratitude to God by loving God and neighbor?_____

_____

What might you have to remove from your routine in order to make room for rhythm?_____

_____

18

Reflection: Personal Action Plan

IN THIS CHAPTER, the homes are listed in the order presented in this book. Of course, you will work on them in the order you determined in the last chapter. If you need to rebuild a home, start there, and then get that home into the Remodel category. Then continue to work on it until you can move it to the Redecorate category and finally the Appreciate category. If you need to Remodel a home, you can skip the Rebuild section below and start with the Remodel section. Work on that home until you can move it to the Redecorate category and then to the Appreciate category. If a home only needs to be Redecorated, you can start there.

As you read the summary of each of the homes below and go through your notes from the reflections, make a list of action items in the space provided. The first items on the list should be the ones from Rebuilding that home, if necessary. Then the next items on the list should be the ones from remodeling and then finally redecorating that home. This is your "to do" list for that particular home, and as you check off the items in the list, you will be building that home and bringing it closer to the Appreciate category.

The point is to work on one home at a time until that home can be moved into the Appreciate category. Only then, move on to the next home on your list. If you try to work on more than one home at a time, you risk defeating the purpose of segmenting your life into the five areas, and you may fall back into chaos because you will be overwhelmed, which leads to the temptation to procrastinate. It's important to see your progress and enjoy the improvements you will make along the way. Therefore, be sure to work on only one home at a time. Work on that home until you can give thanks for it, and then move on to the next home. When you have moved all five homes into the Appreciate category...celebrate!

A HOME FOR YOUR HANDS

Begin by rereading your reflections in chapter three. What stands out as important? What themes or patterns emerge as you look at your notes? How do these themes or patterns connect or compare with your priorities as you wrote them down in the last chapter? Now let's turn your reflections into an action plan.

What does your job do for you now (not just in terms of retirement, but in terms of lifestyle)?

_____

Is your job energizing you or draining you? _____

Does your job negatively affect your life outside of work? _____

Do you live in fear of losing your job because of your performance? _____

If you need to rebuild or remodel the home for your hands...

Start by remembering that your identity is not in your job—you are not your work! If you are married, include your spouse in the decision-making process at each step along the way.

Use the list you made of your Gifts of the Spirit along with the questions above to determine whether you need to change to a different type of job (field) or simply change to a different situation. If you truly need to change fields, what field(s) would be better for you? What kind of job would use as many of your gifts and talents as possible, so that your occupation could be as close as possible to your secondary vocation? How do you want to contribute to the world? Think about the stress continuum and make a list of possible jobs that would give you the right balance of challenge and reward so that you can live without too much stress, and so that your job does not prevent you from having a peaceful life outside of work. Make a short list of a range of jobs or occupations that would allow you to be fulfilled in your work. Don't filter them by salary, but include jobs that would mean you might get paid less than you are used to making.

If you currently have a job, don't quit until you have a concrete offer with a starting date from another employer. Step one is to update your resume so that you have something to give people when the opportunity arises. Create a cover letter that summarizes your skills. If you are currently working, it is advisable to include in the cover letter a request that potential employers not contact your current employer. If possible, get at least one letter of recommendation to include with your resume. There are many books on how to put together a good resume and cover letter. Get some resources from your local public library or get some help and work toward creating a resume and cover letter that you can be proud of. You should be able to do this within a week or two.

If a job you want requires specialized training or more education, now is the time to make a plan to get that training or education. How much will it cost, and how will you pay for it? How much time will it take? Can you keep your current job while going through the training, or will you need to find an intermediate job? Before making a commitment to the training or education, make sure there is a reasonable expectation of finding a job in that field when you are finished.

The next step is to start looking for possible job openings. This is the time to decide whether you may need to move to a new location. If building a home for your body requires a move from your present house or apartment, take this into consideration. Start telling people you trust who are in your (desired) field that you are looking and that they should let you know if they hear of any openings. Take every interview you can get, even if you're not sure whether the job is for you. At the very least, you learn things about the field—and about yourself—from every interview you have.

Remember that you don't owe anyone an explanation why you are changing jobs, except to say that you will be happier after making the change. If the change means you will live in a smaller house, drive a more modest car, or shop at less exclusive stores, just know that your lower level of stress will cause you to outlive all those who might think you're crazy!

If you are redecorating the home for your hands…

Whether or not you need to find a new job, chances are you may need to make some changes related to your work and finances. Do you have debt that causes you stress? Are there any major possessions you could get rid of that would remove loan payments, such as a second home, third car, boat, or timeshare? Would downsizing your home or trading in one of your cars help? What possible changes did you write down in the reflection in chapter three that you might be willing to implement? Are there other lifestyle changes that would reduce your stress and bring more peace? Could you work fewer hours (even if it means getting paid less)? Could you set some boundaries that protect family time, such as setting aside Sundays as the day for the family? Are there any commitments you have that you could get out of to free up time and energy? What else might you do to simplify your life?

Decide which lifestyle changes you will make. Now make a list of the steps you will need to take to make such change(s) a reality. Take the first step within the week.

Walk the Earth: Focusing on the Journey

Don't forget to live while you work. Allow yourself time to enjoy life now, not waiting until later to experience the benefits of your hard work. Think of wealth in terms of lifestyle, not in terms of net worth or even standard of living. What you are buying for you and your family with all that hard work is a lifestyle, so don't sacrifice the lifestyle for the sake of some ideal standard of living. If you have to change your standard of living in order to give yourself a peaceful and healthy lifestyle, do it, and don't make any apology for it.

Being Goldilocks: Looking for the Middle Way

On the other hand, don't live so much for today that you fail to plan for the future. Not putting away enough for retirement can create its own kind of stress. I think that the balance of enjoying life now while planning for the future can be found if you think in terms of simplifying life and evening out your lifestyle now with your intended retirement lifestyle. In other words, don't live like a pauper now to live like a king later, but also don't live like a king now and force yourself to live like a pauper later. Try to live a lifestyle now that you can maintain in retirement with as smooth a transition as possible. Many people find it helpful to consult a financial advisor. As long as you explain to him or her that you are looking for a balance of short term happiness and long term happiness, he or she will be able to give you some guidance on how you can live a modest lifestyle now that will continue into retirement. In this way, you should be able to balance peace (lower stress) now with peace of mind about the future.

Stepping Stones: Establishing Rhythm and Pausing to Breathe

Remember to incorporate rhythms that give you time to stop and think and live intentionally. The work week already has a regular rhythm built into it. It is called the weekend. Make sure you have a weekend. Not all jobs are Monday through Friday, but make sure that you have some time off of work each week to spend time with friends and family. You may think you're getting ahead by working extra hours, but you're not gaining anything—you are only trading your life now for something later—something that may not materialize. If you have to work two jobs or extra hours to pay for education or just to put food on the table, you still need to make some time for rest or you will burn out. Fun is not a luxury—it clears your head so you can do better at your job when you go back to work. Therefore, make sure you schedule time for relaxation, fun, worship, and prayer.

Just as you need to stop and breathe in your days and weeks, you also need to stop and breathe in your months and years. Don't ever let vacation days go to waste. If your employers want to pay you not to work, then by all means, take them up on it. Even if you just take a day to watch movies, do it! If you can travel, then get away and do something different and exciting. If not, take time off to work on your other homes! Finally, I recommend taking a spiritual retreat, maybe once a year.

Home for My Hands: A "To Do" List

1) _____

2) _____

3) _____

4) _____

5) _____

6) _____

7) _____

8) _____

9) _____

10) _____

A HOME FOR YOUR BODY

Begin by rereading your reflections in chapter six. What stands out as important? What themes or patterns emerge as you look at your notes? How do these themes or patterns connect or compare with your priorities and pastimes as you wrote them down in the last chapter? Now let's turn your reflections into an action plan.

Is your house or apartment a place that reduces stress or increases stress? _____

Are you able to rest and recharge your emotional, mental, and spiritual batteries? _____

_____

Is your bedroom too busy to let you sleep? _____

If you need to rebuild the home for your body...

What reasons do you have for wanting to move? Is the house too big and causing stress because of the mortgage? Perhaps it's just too big to keep it clean. Or maybe there are painful memories associated with the house—it's OK if you just need a fresh start. Are you living in a city or climate that is not conducive to your happiness? Based on your reflections, do you just need to move to a different house or apartment or to a different type of home (such as from a house to a townhome or a condo)? Or do you need to move to a different part of town or a different city altogether?

Step one is to start doing some research on where you want to live. Make it fun by going to the bookstore and getting some maps or books on different places. Start making a list of places where you would be happy to live. If possible, take a road trip and drive around different areas to see what they look like. Go on the Internet and see what it costs to buy or rent in different places. If you are married, it would be best for you and your spouse to do this together. If you can't do it together, keep your spouse updated on your thoughts, but make it clear that you won't make any decisions without discussing it and that any decisions that affect you both will be made together.

The realities of employment, the economy, and the housing market may prevent you from moving as soon as you would like to. Even if you can't move right now, start making a plan by choosing some places where you might want to live. If you plan to change cities, you may need to also find a new home for your hands by getting a new job in the new city. As I mentioned above, don't just quit your job and get on a bus. Find a new job in the new city first, and only then should you quit your present job. On the other hand, your present job may allow you to telecommute, or they may have offices in other cities. You should check on that without telling your current employer too much about your plans to move. Once you make a plan, you can create a timeline or a schedule of when you want to put the plan into action. Give yourself specific dates so you have deadlines to work toward. But of course, don't be too hard on yourself if you don't meet those deadlines. Remember that life is a journey, and you can't postpone living and enjoying life until all your homes are perfectly built.

If you are remodeling the home for your body...

Don't be afraid to make some major changes in your home. Can you make new space by changing the purpose of one or more rooms? Rearrange some furniture; put some color on the walls. Throw a painting party, invite your friends, and get some pizza. Don't be afraid of color! Choose

117

colors that seem peaceful, inviting, and happy, but be careful of colors that are too dark, or you may decrease the amount of light in a room and make it seem gloomy. If you do like darker colors, you will need more lighting in that space.

If you have the money to do some remodeling (without going into debt), go for it. But this should not become a burden. Real remodeling can become a long-term project, so only do it if you're ready for that. The point of this is really to rethink your home and be intentional about every space. Do you have what you need to make your home a place that decreases your stress? Make sure to think about your bedroom and wherever it is you like to relax. It may not be a good idea to have a home office in your bedroom, since you will be confronted with work every time you go in there.

If you are redecorating the home for your body...

Get your house ready for sale, and then keep it! If you can afford it, you can actually hire a home stager or realtor to help you see your home through someone else's eyes. The most important thing is to get rid of the clutter. Think of it as the biggest spring cleaning ever. Are there any rooms with piles of stuff you've been meaning to go through? Is there a home office with boxes or stacks of papers you need to deal with? Now is the time to do it. Set aside a day, and don't stop until it's done. Go through the rooms one at a time and strip each room down to its bare essentials, even if you have to move all your belongings into the basement or garage temporarily. Once you have a room stripped bare, start bringing things back in, but be very intentional about whether things really belong where they were. Some things will end up in a different place (possibly including furniture). Some things will end up in the garbage or go to charity. Get rid of as much as possible.

Remember to think of your house or apartment as your own Bat Cave or dollhouse. Only include what you (and your spouse, if you're married) want in it. Remember to decorate for all five senses. Finally, think about where you might add a few reminders of your relationship with God. Is there room for a cross or crucifix on the wall? What about an icon or painting of some biblical scene or a framed Bible verse or inspirational message? Take a trip to your local Christian bookstore and browse around. Don't forget to pick up some CDs while you're there.

Walk the Earth: Focusing on the Journey

As you remodel or redecorate the home for your body, find a place for everything, and as much as possible, put everything in its place. Remember to treat yourself like company and keep things put away, cleaning as you go so that you can enjoy a more peaceful house. Also, when company does come over, it's not such a big job to get the place ready.

Being Goldilocks: Looking for the Middle Way

Finding the happy medium in a home for your body is all about living in-between the extremes of chaos and museum. You shouldn't be stepping over things just to walk around the house, but on the other hand, you shouldn't live with plastic covers on everything, either. The home for your body should be characterized by comfort but not luxury, relaxed but not messy. If you are naturally a messy person, this may be the time to work on some new habits. On the other hand, if you are naturally a neat freak, it may be time to loosen up. I'm not suggesting major personality changes, just enough to make your house more relaxing and comfortable. Find the happy medium.

Being Goldilocks also means finding the right temperature—not too hot, not too cold.

It means a balance of going out and staying in. Learn to cook good food at home, so you don't have to go out to get a good meal and so the place smells good. You shouldn't have to leave your house to relax.

Stepping Stones: Establishing Rhythm and Pausing to Breathe

Allow yourself to watch television when it helps you relax, but don't have the TV on all the time. Be intentional about when it's on. In other words, having the TV on can be like a pause between the stepping stones, but don't let it become more than that. Make a list of shows you can't live without and enjoy them, but don't just channel surf. As a default, opt for music rather than television if it's only going to be in the background.

Home for My Body: A "To Do" List

1) _____

2) _____

3) _____

4) _____

5) _____

6) _____

7) _____

8) _____

9) _____

10) _____

A HOME FOR YOUR MIND

Begin by rereading your reflections in chapter nine. What stands out as important? What themes or patterns emerge as you look at your notes? How do these themes or patterns connect or compare with your priorities, passions, and pastimes, as you wrote them down in the last chapter? Now let's turn your reflections into an action plan.

Is there a part of you that is stifled or suppressed? _____

What gifts/talents are not being used at work? _____

_____

What are your passions? _____

_____

If you need to rebuild the home for your mind...

Based on your reflection and your answers to the questions above, what parts of your personality or what gifts or talents are not currently finding expression in your life? Make a list of specific activities that would allow you to express yourself in these ways. Pick one of these activities as your first choice. Is there a club or league you can join that would enable you to schedule regular activity? In other words, if you feel that you are not able to express some artistic or productive side of you, is there a class you could take to enhance your skills and meet others who are interested in the same things? Or if you are interested in some sport or other activity, are there lessons you can take or a league you can join that would obligate you to show up and be part of a class or team once a week or so? Make a plan to take those classes or lessons or to join that league. Whatever it is, make the commitment and stick to it.

If you are overweight, see your doctor about a diet and exercise plan. If you are struggling with unhealthy habits or addictions, or if you are finding it hard to let go of anger and resentment, it is possible that you need to seek help from a mental health professional. What steps would you need to take to begin this process? Check into your employer's insurance program to see if such help is covered by your insurance. Check the list of doctors/therapists and find one in your area. Make an appointment to talk with this person. Remember that by making one appointment, you are not obligated to continue seeing this person. Just commit to one hour and see how it goes.

The point here is that if you need to rebuild the home for your mind, you need to do two things: you need to get involved in something active, and you need to cultivate healthy habits. It may be that you can do both of these with one activity such as a sport or other exercise. Just remember, no matter who you are and no matter what you choose to do to express your creativity, everyone needs exercise!

If you are remodeling the home for your mind...

What are your passions? What is your favorite passion or pastime? How can you plan to spend more time on this? What steps would you have to take to make more time for this? What club, group, or league would you have to join that would make you schedule time for this and keep that commitment? How can you simplify your life to make more time for the things that relax you? Are there any old commitments you can get rid of to make time for new, healthier, commitments?

Are you happy with your state of physical fitness? If not, how many pounds would you need to lose to be happy and healthy? If in doubt, err on the side of losing fewer pounds and weighing a little more. Unless the home for your hands is *supermodel*, you probably don't need to live up to anyone else's standards of perfection. Just work toward the weight that makes you feel good physically. If you're trying to lose weight to feel good emotionally, then you should check in with your doctor or a counselor since you may have an unrealistic expectation of what you should look like. If you lose enough weight to drop a few inches from your waist or go down a dress size, celebrate by buying some new clothes, and don't keep the bigger clothes—give them to charity.

If you are redecorating the home for your mind...

Remember that there are two types of activities: exercise and creative expression. Make sure you have both kinds in your life. It's fine if one thing such as a sports league or the study of martial arts includes both exercise and creative expression, as long as you have both. Also remember that creative expression can be active or passive. There is nothing wrong with passive expression. If you really like time travel movies and discussing the hypothetical implications of time travel with your friends, that may be a great way to relax. But then you will need something else to give you some exercise. The point is to make time for both relaxing (creative expression) and exercise. Your mind needs both.

Walk the Earth: Focusing on the Journey

A healthy body and a healthy mind are interrelated. Therefore, the home for your mind includes your body. If you are out of shape, or if your mind is clouded with addictions or other bad habits, you will not have the clarity you need to make good decisions and live intentionally. This kind of mental clarity is also essential in resisting temptation. For example, when I've already eaten an entire pizza, there is no way I'm going to be able to pass up the cookies. I know, you would think I'd be full, but it doesn't work that way, at least not for me. On the other hand, when I've been able to keep up better eating habits and exercise, it's a lot easier to resist the cookies. This can become a vicious cycle if you get to feeling down on yourself because of your eating habits, so do your best to be at your best. Good habits breed more good habits, but a defeated attitude leads to giving up. Also, if

you are constantly frustrated with feeling that your creativity is suppressed or if parts of your personality remain unexpressed, the frustration will begin to affect your judgment.

Living life as a journey means you can't live in the past, as if the time when you used to be in shape makes up for being overweight or underactive now. It also means you can't only live for the future, as if life will really start when you reach a certain dress or pants size or when you reach a certain skill level. Learn to accept yourself as you are, without excusing yourself from personal improvement.

Being Goldilocks: Looking for the Middle Way

Focusing on the journey means looking for the healthy and happy medium today—right now. Sometimes that means recognizing that you can't wait for health and happiness to come to you. It requires discipline. Being Goldilocks is being willing to give up some short-term fun to get long-term health and happiness. In other words, sometimes you have to get off the couch and go out and get some exercise. The balance is finding the right amount of couch time. Too much couch time means not enough exercise. But too little couch time is not good, either, since just as everyone needs exercise—everyone needs to relax.

Being Goldilocks also has to do with balancing your self-image. It's about finding the balance of a healthy self-esteem with a healthy humility. It's the middle way between thinking too highly of yourself (pride) and thinking too little of yourself. Therefore, be careful not to let yourself think you are fine the way you are without any creative or physical activity, but also be careful not to think your value as a person has anything to do with your physical fitness. Physical fitness is only for the purpose of feeling good and living long, not for measuring up to anyone else's standards. That also means that you can't afford to mentally beat yourself up if you don't measure up to some standard of your own. As long as you're doing *something* and trying to incorporate both kinds of activity in your life, then you are moving in the right direction.

Stepping Stones: Establishing Rhythm and Pausing to Breathe

When you put the home for your hands and the home for your mind together, hopefully you will find opportunities to use most or all of your gifts and talents and to be creative and/or productive. Then it becomes a matter of establishing a healthy rhythm of work and play (relaxation)

time. You will want to make sure that you allow yourself enough time to work on your passion(s), without feeling guilty that you're not getting work done. Some people are so driven that relaxing can actually cause stress because they feel like they should be accomplishing something. If you're like me, you tend to think you won't be able to relax until all the work is done. But the truth is, all the work is never done. When you get to heaven, then all the work will be done. In the meantime, try to train yourself to be OK with putting work aside and give yourself permission to play. This means a little every day, if possible, but certainly every week. When you play and relax, you *are* accomplishing something—you are recharging the batteries for when you get back to work. On the other hand, some people are naturally procrastinators, putting off the work until the fun is done. But that's the opposite problem, since most people could find enough fun things to do to postpone working forever. Establishing a rhythm of appropriate amounts of work and play is the way to finding the balance that will allow you to be happy living the journey.

Home for My Mind: A "To Do" List

1) _____

2) _____

3) _____

4) _____

5) _____

6) _____

7) _____

8) _____

9) _____

10) _____

A HOME FOR YOUR HEART

Begin by rereading your reflections in chapter twelve. What stands out as important? What themes or patterns emerge as you look at your notes? How do these themes or patterns connect or compare with your priorities as you wrote them down in the last chapter? Now let's turn your reflections into an action plan.

Remember that the meaning of life is in relationships. We all need unconditional love, acceptance, and companionship, and though love is a risk, the risk is worth it. By being quick to apologize and quick to forgive, we are helping our loved ones build the homes for their hearts, homes in which it is safe to be wrong and safe to apologize, and in turn we are building the home for our own heart.

If you need to rebuild the home for your heart...

If you are married, and you feel that your marriage is not a safe home for your heart, you probably need to get professional help. See if your church can recommend a professional marriage counselor, or find one in your community. It may be that your employer's insurance will cover this kind of therapy, and if so, your insurance plan may have a list of therapists from which to choose. Make a commitment to check on the insurance and get the list of doctors within a week. Then choose one and make your first appointment as soon as possible. If your spouse will not go with you, go alone and get the process started.

If you are single, start by making some new friendships, and put off looking for a significant other until all your other homes are in the Appreciate category. Start by thinking about the home for your mind, and combine efforts in terms of joining a sports league or taking classes or lessons. When you make time for your passions by joining with a group for that specific purpose, you will automatically meet people who are interested in the same things you are. You can also combine efforts with the home for your spirit by getting involved in a church and making new friends there. Make as many new friends as possible. At first you will want to join in with groups of friends, but with time you will come to realize that you are closer to certain friends, and you can begin doing things in smaller groups and one-on-one. If you belong to multiple groups, you can introduce your new friends in one group to your new friends in another group. That way, you are all new friends, and no one feels singled out.

If you are remodeling the home for your heart…

If you are married, go through the job description of a husband or wife as outlined in chapter twelve. With each one, ask yourself if you are fulfilling that part of your job description. This is not the time to evaluate your spouse—remember that if you want a lover, you have to *be* a lover. Are you serving your spouse, or are you serving yourself most of the time? Note the items on the job description list that you could do better. Make a plan to work on these in your marriage. By getting better at your job description, you will create a good home for your spouse's heart, and you will improve the home for your heart in the process. If your spouse is willing, you might also go over the job description with your spouse and ask him or her whether there are any you could work on—just be careful that it doesn't seem like a set-up as if you started the conversation so you could complain about him or her. Talk together about whether you both are happy with the amount of quality time spent together. Also talk about what constitutes "quality" time. Your definitions might not be the same!

If you are single, go back to the list you made of your friends, as well as the list of your best friends or your "inner circle." You made some notes on how you could show appreciation for your friendship. Make a plan to do something for one or more of your friends. You could throw a party, but it doesn't have to be that elaborate. You could invite them to dinner and cook for them. Or if you're not into cooking, invite them over for takeout and a movie on DVD. You could plan to go shopping with one or more friends or simply out to lunch. Whatever it is, make a list of anything you need to do to make this happen. Take the first step this week. In the future, don't wait for them to call you. The reality is that in many friendships, one person calls more than the other. That doesn't necessarily mean one person likes the other more. It simply means one person has taken on the role of event planner. If that's you (or if no one has taken that role until now), take it and embrace it. Mark your calendar once a month or once a week (whatever feels right) to call and make plans with this or that friend or group. If it has to be up to you to be the social coordinator, so be it. At least you won't be sitting home alone.

If you are redecorating the home for your heart...

If you are married, talk with your spouse about the amount of time you spend together and the kinds of things you do that count as quality time. Are you both happy with the amount of time spent together and with the kinds of activities you do together? Remember that sometimes you may need to do things that are not your first choice in order for your spouse to be able to enjoy your time together. Are you both happy with the amount of time spent with friends and with the particular friends you choose to spend time with? Are there any people in your life who create conflict between you and your spouse? If so, talk about how you can move the person or people in question off to the periphery of your life. Decrease the time spent with people who are catalysts for negative emotions.

Spend some time talking with your spouse about your hopes for the future. Remember, don't be a dream-killer, and if your spouse seems fearful about any of your hopes or dreams, reassure him or her that you're in this together and that being together is more important than realizing any dreams or accomplishing any goals. Talk about what it means to serve each other and have a Servant-Servant marriage. Also remember to listen unselfishly every day. Make a pact to act like newlyweds forever. Now make a plan to put each other first, and put that plan on the calendar. Do you need to schedule regular time alone? Do you need to schedule regular fun activities together? Do you need to schedule regular time with friends—or do you need to decrease time spent with some people? Your calendar is your greatest tool here, so don't be afraid to use it. It is not unromantic to plan ahead for a date night or other quality time!

If you are single, the same applies to you with regard to your calendar. It is the best tool for making sure you balance time spent alone and time spent with friends. The way that you can make sure to spend your life doing the things you want to do is to plan ahead. Of course, some things come up at the last minute, so it's good to remain flexible and not over-schedule yourself. In fact, it's a good idea to block out some time alone so that you make sure you balance your social time with time to rest and think. Everyone needs a different amount of time alone, but everyone should have some time alone at least once in a while. It might be once a day, once a week, or only once a month. Don't be afraid of trial and error—experiment to figure out how much time alone is right for you. Then put it on the calendar so you don't cheat yourself out of the relaxation that you need. Of course, if something comes up at the last minute and you get invited to a party or other social event, it's up to you whether you want to forego your alone time or say that you have another commitment.

Think about your closest relationships, friends, and relatives. Which ones energize you and which ones drain you? Why do you think some relationships drain you? Is there some imbalance in the relationship, making you feel as though you give more than you get? Do you feel taken advantage of? It's good to take the position of a servant, even with your friends. However, if you have relationships that drain you emotionally, it might be a good idea to think about decreasing the amount of time spent with those people—even if they are relatives. Plan to spend more time with the people who energize you. With those people, chances are you can be a servant without being taken advantage of.

Walk the Earth: Focusing on the Journey

In all of our relationships (including our relationship with God), our life and our behavior is best when it is motivated by gratitude. Gratitude means counting your blessings and realizing that most of the time we get far more than we deserve. Therefore, gratitude leads to humility. Remember that humility is being satisfied with what you have but unsatisfied with the way you are. You don't complain about your circumstances, but you realize there is room for growth in your life. This is the opposite of pride, which takes the attitude that you deserve more than you have, and you're already the best you can be. In any given situation, we might think that we would be happier if we could assert ourselves with an attitude of entitlement and get our way, but the truth is that humility, not pride, leads to happiness. This is because humility allows us to be compassionate and forgiving with others, which promotes loving relationships. And the meaning of life is in those relationships.

So gratitude leads to humility, and humility leads to servanthood. Remember that you can't get what you want by trying to get what you want.

It's ironic, but true. You can only be fulfilled in life by being in fulfilling relationships. And the only way to have fulfilling relationships is to be a servant and accept people as they are. This will motivate them to want to grow themselves and even to serve you. The other irony is that people only feel free to grow when they feel it is safe to be themselves. They only feel safe to serve when they aren't afraid of being taken advantage of. But when the snowball is rolling down the right side of the hill, people truly can bring out the best in each other.

Being Goldilocks: Looking for the Middle Way

Of course being a servant only works if the other person in the relationships can resist the temptation to take advantage of your servanthood. That's why I say that if there are relationships that drain you or people in your life who create negative emotion, the best thing to do is decrease the time spent with those people and especially time spent alone with those people. Pray for them, but don't subject yourself to destructive or unhealthy behaviors.

However, sometimes loving your neighbor means entering into a relationship that will be one-sided. Sometimes people find themselves in a situation where they cannot be in a mutual relationship of servanthood. In the Parable of the Good Samaritan, the injured man was in no position to do anything but accept the service of the Samaritan. Any time we feed the hungry or help the poor, or even lead a group or organization, we are not looking for a relationship, but we are engaged in ministry. There is a difference, and it's important to keep that in mind. Some people find that they do get certain needs met by ministering to others. However, it would be unhealthy to substitute ministry (unequal) relationships for real friendship. Being Goldilocks means cultivating healthy equal relationships, not substituting unequal relationships to meet one's relational needs. It means balancing time spent alone and time spent with friends, and balancing serving others with taking care of oneself.

Stepping Stones: Establishing Rhythm and Pausing to Breathe

In many social relationships, there is already a built-in rhythm. You see your coworkers during the day, but you get a break from them in the evenings. You see your friends on the weekends, but you may not see them much during the week. Remember that this is a good thing, but if you're working too much, you may be spending too much time with coworkers and not enough time with friends. If you are going out every night, you may be spending too much time with friends and not enough time alone. If you are married and you only let the routines of the week dictate your schedule, you may be forgetting to plan quality time with your spouse, such as a regular date night. Use your calendar to be intentional about your social rhythms. Go through your list of friends and note how often you think would be the ideal frequency to see each one. How far from the ideal are you now? How can you rearrange your schedule to get closer to the ideal? Just keep in mind that your ideal might not be the same as theirs, so if that's the case, work toward a compromise, and don't take it personally if you're not everyone's best friend. We're looking for balance, not perfection. Get as close to the ideal as you can, and just enjoy each day as it comes.

Home for My Heart: A "To Do" List

1) _____

2) _____

3) _____

4) _____

5) _____

6) _____

7) _____

8) _____

9) _____

10) _____

A HOME FOR YOUR SPIRIT

Begin by rereading your reflections in chapter fifteen. What stands out as important? What themes or patterns emerge as you look at your notes? How do these themes or patterns connect or compare with your priorities and passions, as you wrote them down in the last chapter? How might your gifts and talents give you a doorway into a church—in other words, what can you offer a church in terms of ministry skills? Now let's turn your reflections into an action plan.

Remember to embrace mystery. If a church claims to have all the answers, it only means they haven't asked all the questions. The point is to belong to something greater than yourself—not just a local church, but the universal Church, and the communion of saints. Remember that your connection to the Church sits on the "spiritual tripod" with three legs: corporate worship, personal devotion, and social responsibility.

If you need to rebuild the home for your spirit…

You already know that I believe very strongly that a person cannot live up to his or her potential as a human being or be truly fulfilled in life without a relationship with God. As Christians, we believe that our relationship with God is made possible by Christ and is realized through Christ. Furthermore, we identify with Christ through his body the Church. This means that local church membership is not optional. It is a must, and there is no way around it. Especially if you feel that you are cut off from God and need reconciliation, it is through the Church that you will find that reconciliation with God. If your feelings of alienation from God are due to anger or resentment that you are holding, it is essential that you deal with this or it will always short-circuit your attempts to connect with God. Dealing with anger or resentment may require making an appointment with a pastor, counselor, or therapist. Even though it may be hard to take the first step toward getting this kind of help, you will be a happier person after you do.

Finding a church can be frustrating, but it can also be fun. Get a map of your town, and find the spot where you live. Make that point the center and draw a circle, with a radius equal to the amount of distance you are willing to drive at least once a week. I suggest making that circle as small as possible, so that your church will be part of your neighborhood. If you have a particular denominational affiliation in your family background, start with that. Find any church(es) of that denomination within your circle. Plan to visit all of them. If there are only one or two, don't be too quick to judge on one visit. Go back to each one at least twice. If there are no churches of your own denomination within the circle, see if you could get to one by making the circle a little wider. If not, you may need to try something different. We can't go into all the different Christian denominations here, but remember to think like Goldilocks when you are visiting a church. Look for balance, and avoid the extremes. Look for a church that honors the Scriptures but does not idolize them. Look for a church that upholds the ancient traditions and remains connected to the historic Church but is relevant in the present. Look for a church that emphasizes all three legs of the spiritual tripod. Finally, look for a church that affirms both the real humanity and the full divinity of Jesus Christ. Any church or group that denies or de-emphasizes one or the other is living on the fringe. Remember, the truth is in the middle.

Unfortunately, most churches are not very good at welcoming visitors. If you visit a church and no one talks to you, don't take it personally. They may have failed at making you feel welcome, but don't write them off. It doesn't necessarily mean it's not a friendly church or that the people aren't nice. It just means they have not yet organized a welcoming ministry. It may be up to you to take the initiative to introduce yourself to people, but it will be worth it.

Once you find a church, become a member. Don't just attend worship and go home. You won't feel like you're part of the church until you get to know the people, which is hard to do if you only go to weekend services. You will eventually need to get involved beyond just Sunday morning if you want to make friends in the church.

If you are remodeling or redecorating the home for your spirit...

Get a bulletin from your church or go to the church's Web site. Look at the worship services that are offered and the days and times. Personally, I'm a big fan of the evening service, because I like to sleep late on Sundays. I know it doesn't sound like a very spiritual motivation to pick a service, but that's OK. If you hate getting up on Sundays, that is no longer an excuse to miss church, because most churches have Saturday afternoon or evening services or perhaps even Sunday late afternoon services. Once you see what your options are, pick the service that makes the most sense to you. Some churches have a different kind of music or worship style at different services. Pick the one that will be "your" service. This is important, because if you float around, going to different services whenever you go, you won't see the same people each week. In fact, in larger churches, the different services can function like smaller separate church congregations. The point here is to pick one and commit to it. That doesn't mean you can't switch once in a while if you have something else you want to do on that day, but make that the exception to the rule. Pick a service, and put it on your calendar for every week. This is your service, and the people you will see there every week are your brothers and sisters in Christ. Start going regularly, and try to notice the other people. When you've seen the same people a few times, introduce yourself.

Think about your prayer life. Do you talk to God enough outside of church? Do you ever just sit and listen to God? When you're in prayer, if you take time to be quiet, God will speak to you. Not out loud (probably), but within your spirit, in your conscience, or in your mind. Do you share the good times with God in thanksgiving, not just the problems? Do you pray enough? How much is enough for you? If you were to pray more often, when would it be? In the morning, so you can start your day with God? In the evening, so you can thank God for the day? What seems best for you? Start experimenting with different times and frequency of prayer. Figure out if it works for you to pray twice a week, once a day, or several times a day. Figure out what time of day works best for you. Do you see where this is going? Yes—put it on your calendar. I know, it will look a little strange if someone sees your calendar, but that's only because the values of the world are backwards compared to the values of the kingdom of God. Put reminders to pray on your calendar, and keep doing that until you don't need reminders any more. Try not to let it become a routine or a burden, though. Make it a rhythm of your life to stop and talk to God regularly. If you don't know what to say to God, read my pamphlet, *Pray (Not Just Say) the Lord's Prayer*. It will help you customize your time of prayer so that it's personal, spontaneous, and meaningful.

Finally, when you have the other two legs to your tripod (regular worship attendance and regular prayer outside of worship), it's time to attend to the third leg of the tripod—social responsibility. Your church probably has a list somewhere of all the groups that meet and the ministries that take place. Get that list. Go through the list and see what groups exist for people like you. Are there meetings for certain age groups? Singles or married couples? Write down anything that describes you as a possible group to join. Now go back to your list of spiritual gifts and talents. Match your gifts, talents, and passions with any of the ministries that exist to help others. Wherever there is a match, in other words, any ministries that could use your help, write those down. Now you have a list of groups and ministries of the church where you would fit in. Pick one, and sign up. Don't be afraid of trial and error here, too. There is nothing wrong with trying something for a while and then moving on. You are not taking a vow or making a lifelong commitment. Just try something. Eventually, work your way up to at least one social group and at least one ministry.

Walk the Earth: Focusing on the Journey

As you focus on the journey and leave the destination up to God, also focus on extending grace and mercy to others and leave the justice up to God. Live every day motivated by gratitude for the love and forgiveness that God has extended to you, and then be patient with others and be quick to forgive them. It is liberating to give up the responsibility of being your own higher power and submit to God. Live the paradox of finding freedom in submission and security through surrender. True peace comes from entrusting yourself—not to your own abilities or your own resources—but to God.

Being Goldilocks: Looking for the Middle Way

Being Goldilocks in our spirituality means finding the balance of service and devotion in our lives. We need to be engaged in both social responsibility and devotion. And when it comes to devotion, we need both kinds: corporate worship and personal (private) prayer. Remember the two beams of the cross, the vertical beam (loving God) and the horizontal beam (loving neighbor). Your life as a Christian is incomplete unless you have both beams. But also remember that there is a logical priority that encounter with God must precede social action. The story of Martha and Mary (see Luke 10:38–42) shows that Mary had *chosen the better part*, meaning that the (vertical) relationship with God must be primary, because you can't give what you don't have.

Being Goldilocks also means avoiding the extremes when it comes to both belief and practice. As I mentioned, avoid any teachers who emphasize the humanity of Christ and ignore his divinity. But also avoid any teachers who emphasize the divinity of Christ and ignore his humanity. True Christianity accepts both the full humanity and the full divinity of Christ. (For more on this, see my book, *The Earliest Christologies: Trinitarian Orthodoxy Before Nicaea.*) Avoid teachers who say there is no such thing as sin, but also avoid teachers who say that you should hate anyone or that you should stop seeing your friends and loved ones because they have a different kind of spirituality. The truth is in the middle: sin is a reality, but Christ never advocated isolating yourself from people. Remember that by virtue of our baptism, we are all ministers of the Gospel, commissioned with the ministry of reconciliation. In 2 Corinthians 5:18–20, the Apostle Paul said that since God has reconciled us to himself through Christ, we should also be extending the invitation of reconciliation with God in Christ to others. The gifts and the love of God must be shared, or we disrespect the Giver. These are the gifts which must be given away to be kept, and to try to keep them to ourselves will ultimately end in losing them.

Stepping Stones: Establishing Rhythm and Pausing to Breathe

You can't sing a whole song in one breath, so don't try to live a whole week, or even a whole day, without stopping to breathe, to pray, and to think so you can live your life intentionally. Remember that rhythm is holy, and rhythm allows you to stop, connect to the divine power Source, and recharge your mental, emotional, and spiritual batteries. Make your prayer life a rhythm but not a routine, a breath but not a burden. The ideal rhythm might include something like this: Daily Prayer, Weekly Worship, Monthly Service projects, and an Annual Retreat. But no matter what kind of rhythm works for you, it's all about stopping regularly to count your blessings, to express your gratitude to God, and to be self-aware. Then live every day and make every decision out of that gratitude and self-awareness. If you can do this, you will be happier, and so will everyone around you.

Home for My Spirit: A "To Do" List

1) _____

2) _____

3) _____

4) _____

5) _____

6) _____

7) _____

8) _____

9) _____

10) _____

Appendix 1

List of Spiritual Gifts

The **Gifts of the Holy Spirit** are found in 1 Corinthians 12–14, as well as Romans 12 and Ephesians 4. In the list below, the Gifts of the Spirit are presented as categories of spiritual gifts relevant to contemporary work and ministry. Specific talents or abilities are grouped under the categories of Gifts of the Spirit. Circle any talents or abilities that you believe you have. If you can think of talents or abilities that are not on this list, feel free to write them in. If several of the talents or abilities under a certain category apply to you, chances are you have that particular Gift of the Spirit.

ADMINISTRATION

- Accounting/financial planning
- Clerical work
- Computers/database
- Graphic design/layout/desktop publishing
- Legal services
- Management/personnel
- Organizing
- Phone calling
- Photography
- Planning/event planning
- Registration
- Web site design/maintenance

DISCERNMENT
(The Gift of Distinguishing Spirits)

- Analyzing
- Delegating
- Discussing/group process facilitation
- Evaluating
- Interviewing
- Recruiting

EVANGELISM
(The Gift of Apostleship)

- Communication
- Faith sharing/evangelization
- Phone calling

HEALING/COMPASSION
(The Gift of Generosity)

- Caring/compassion
- Listening
- Medical/nursing care
- Nurturing
- Sharing/generosity with resources
- Social justice work
- Visiting the sick or imprisoned

KNOWLEDGE

- Learning/learning languages
- Library work
- Researching
- Summarizing/synthesizing
- Teaching/explaining concepts
- Writing/editing/proofreading

LEADERSHIP
(The Gift of Wisdom)

- Leading and motivating a group
- Mentoring/counseling
- Negotiating
- Problem solving
- Visioning/brain storming

MUSICAL/LITURGICAL EXPRESSION
(The Gift of Psalms)

- Acting/directing of dramatic presentations
- Audio or video systems operation/recording
- Music performance
- Planning or participating in liturgy
- Songwriting/composing/writing lyrics or poetry

PROCLAMATION/EXHORTATION
(The Gift of Prophecy)

- Capital campaign leadership/fundraising
- Marketing/promoting programs/gaining support for ideas
- Public speaking/storytelling
- Sharing ideas, new visions

SERVING/HELPING

- Construction/carpentry/electrical
- Cooking/serving food
- Decorating
- Driving
- Gardening
- Hospitality
- Housekeeping
- Maintenance of building and grounds
- Ministry to people with special needs
- Painting
- Sewing
- Welcoming/reception

SPIRITUALITY/DEVOTION
(The Gift of Faith)

- Creating devotional experiences
- Leading prayer or other devotional experiences
- Meditating
- Praying

TEACHING

- Childcare
- Guiding/facilitating groups, meetings, retreats
- Recreation/sports coaching
- Teaching/training
- Team building
- Youth ministry

Appendix 2
Guided Devotional Experience

TRY TO IMAGINE YOURSELF in the place described below. Once you have done this exercise a few times and you no longer need to read it from the page, you can close your eyes. At that time, feel free to change the experience in any way that is meaningful to you.

It's very hot, and you can feel sand under your feet. You are in a land that would be one hundred degrees in the shade, but there is no shade. You've been walking for miles, and as the afternoon wears on, you are both hopeful and a little fearful. You have been invited to dinner in a home where a teacher from out of town will be the guest of honor. His name is Jesus, and you're hopeful about the message that he will have for the group—but you're afraid that he will look at you and know that you are not as good as you would like to be. When you arrive at the house, the afternoon sun is still high in the sky, and the relief from the heat gives you courage to go inside. You see Jesus, already seated at the far end of the table. You take a seat at the end of the table closest to the door and farthest from Jesus. But Jesus sees and looks right into your eyes. You know you are not worthy to sit at the table with

Jesus, but Jesus speaks your name. Imagine Jesus speaking your name in a gentle and peaceful way.

Jesus walks to you and says, "I'm glad you came." Then he gives you a big tight hug that seems to last forever. Imagine Jesus giving you a hug. Imagine his beard scratching your face. Imagine the rough fabric of his robe. Imagine yourself hugging him back.

Now Jesus takes you by the arm and practically drags you to the head of the table. He asks you to sit by him, and he won't take no for an answer. You protest, trying to find a way to say you don't think you're worthy to sit next to Jesus, but he looks you straight in the eyes as if to say, "I know, but I want you here with me anyway."

During dinner, Jesus teaches about the two greatest commandments—loving God with your *hands, body, mind, heart and spirit*; and loving your neighbor as yourself. As the meal is finished and the evening turns to night, the discussion evolves into several small conversations around the table. Everyone is deep in debate in small groups of two or three, and you find yourself talking with Jesus. Just you and Jesus. Now he looks at you with sincere eyes that seem to ask, "Well…what is it you want to say to me?"

What is it you want to say to Jesus today? Imagine telling Jesus whatever you want him to know, and know that he really does hear you.

Is there anything you want to confess to Jesus? Tell him, because he already knows about it. There is nothing you can say that will shock him, and there is nothing you can tell him that will make him reject you.

Now imagine that Jesus says, "Your sins are forgiven. They are as far from you as the east is from the west."

Is there anything that has you anxious? Share that with Jesus.

Now imagine that Jesus says, "Peace be with you."

What else do you want to talk to Jesus about today? He is here for you, as long as it takes. It doesn't have to be anything of great significance—just whatever is on your mind today. Don't be afraid to imagine a conversation with Jesus, because in imagining it, you're having that conversation with him. But don't forget to listen for him to speak to you, and he will speak to you through his Holy Spirit who is within you. Take as much time as you want to continue to have a conversation with Jesus. When you feel ready to end your conversation with Jesus, thank him for the time spent with him today.

Appendix 3
The Gratitude Rosary

THE GRATITUDE ROSARY is an ecumenical prayer form that uses an ordinary rosary as prayer beads for counting your blessings. Prayer beads have been used by many faiths throughout history as a reminder to pray and as a reminder of things to pray about. The Gratitude Rosary can be used by any Christian, since the prayers are not specific to a particular denomination. In other words, the rosary is not just for Catholics anymore!

The rosary is divided into five *decades*, or segments of ten beads. When praying the Gratitude Rosary, each decade represents one of the five homes. The object is to use the ten beads in each decade to give thanks for ten things that relate to the home in question. The ten things you give thanks for can change every time you pray, or they can be the same ten things each time. With each of the ten beads within a decade, think of one thing you are thankful for, say a short prayer of thanksgiving to God, and dedicate it to God.

The beads that separate the decades can represent any prayer or Scripture reading that is meaningful to you, but I have suggested a few below to get you started.

SUGGESTED METHOD FOR PRAYING THE GRATITUDE ROSARY:

Begin at the cross, meditating on James 4:8: "Draw near to God, and he will draw near to you…"

At the first bead from the cross, repeat the Jesus prayer as many times as needed to make sure that your prayer is Christ-centered: Lord Jesus Christ, Son of God, have mercy on me, a sinner…

At the next three beads, express your thanks to God for the past, your desire to follow and be close to God in the present, and your trust in God for the future.

At the last bead before the circle, meditate on Psalm 46: "Be still, and know that I am God…"

The first decade represents the home for your hands. With each bead, give thanks for some aspect of your job. Even if you hate your job, the object is to find things to be thankful for. Keep everything in perspective relative to the big picture of your destiny—eternal life in the kingdom of God. Keep in mind that no matter how bad it is, it could be worse. If you have a job, be thankful for that. If you are between jobs, be thankful for the ways God provides. Use each of the ten beads to give thanks for one thing so that you count ten blessings related to the home for your hands. After each bead, dedicate whatever you have given thanks for to God. Entrust your future and the future of this particular blessing to God. Say something like: "Lord I thank you for _____; I dedicate it and entrust it to you. Please give me your peace."

At the bead between decades, repeat the words of John the Baptist in John 3:30 as many times as necessary to keep your prayer Christ-centered: "He must increase, but I must decrease…"

Repeat the above steps for each of the five decades, as they each represent one of the five homes. When you complete the circle, you will have given thanks for fifty things. This should help you keep your life in perspective and remind you of all that you have as you work on your homes. It should also help you live your life motivated by gratitude.

When you reach the end of the circle, ask God to help you see all the gifts and invitations that will come your way and to see God in the small details of everyday life.

Appendix 4
Motivational Reminders

HERE ARE SOME short statements taken from the chapters above that will help you remember the lessons you learned from reading this book. I've included some of the ironic truths that we all need to keep in mind, because although they are true, they seem to be counter-intuitive. If we don't consciously try to remember them, our own behavior can work against us. I wish you the best of good fortune and God's blessings as you put these concepts into practice in your life and as you build your five homes.

THE HOME FOR YOUR HANDS

- You have to live while you work.
- It doesn't pay to chase after money.
- What would Goldilocks do (WWGD)?
- Less stress means more peace—live with less, reduce your stress.
- Success is not a goal; it is a lifestyle.
- The only risk of failure is the possibility of looking back on a life that was postponed until it was too late.

THE HOME FOR YOUR BODY

- If your body isn't happy, the rest of you can't be happy, either.
- Learn from the puppies—don't clutter where you live.
- If it looks busy or sounds noisy, it's stressful.
- Get your house ready for sale—then keep it!
- Treat yourself like company.

THE HOME FOR YOUR MIND

- Everyone needs exercise.
- The refusal to forgive is a sin.
- Be self-aware and live intentionally.
- Life is a journey, not a destination.
- There is no standing still; one is either moving closer to God or farther from him.
- It doesn't matter where you've been, only whether you are moving in the right direction.
- Thought leads to action, and repeated action leads to habit—therefore, thinking about good things will lead to good habits.

THE HOME FOR YOUR HEART

- Stop thinking of yourself as a treasure hunter, and start thinking of yourself as the treasure.
- Roll the snowball down the right side of the hill—be quick to apologize and quick to forgive.
- You can't get what you want by trying to get what you want.
- Unselfishness is the best thing you can do for yourself!
- Be a servant but not a doormat.
- Don't be a dream-killer; encourage other people's hopes for the future.
- It is only safe to grow when it's safe to be yourself.
- If you try to change your partner, you will only change him or her into a resentful person.
- It is more important to be on the same side as your spouse than it is to be right.
- Marriage is like an oak tree; it's either growing or dying.

THE HOME FOR YOUR SPIRIT

- Remember the spiritual tripod: corporate worship, personal devotion, social responsibility.
- You can't give what you don't have.
- The gifts and love of God must be shared or we disrespect the Giver.
- The gifts of God must be given away to be kept.
- Suffering is like an echo—rejecting it or reflecting it only prolongs it.

ALL FIVE HOMES

- Your identity will never change: You are a Christian—a child of God, made in the image of God.
- The meaning of life is in relationships of love and acceptance with God, loved ones, and friends.
- Your destiny is eternal life in the kingdom of heaven.
- Peace comes from order and simplicity of life and from focusing on loving relationships.
- Hope comes from living intentionally and being motivated by gratitude.
- Enjoy the journey, and leave the destination up to God.
- Extend forgiveness to all, and leave the justice up to God.
- Humility is being satisfied with what you have but unsatisfied with the way you are.
- Be like Goldilocks—look for the happy medium of balance between the extremes.
- There is no shame in asking for help; a dentist can't drill his own teeth!

Appendix 5

Suggestions and Recommendations

BOOKS EVERYONE SHOULD READ:

The Five Love Languages, by Gary Chapman.

The Seven Principles for Making Marriage Work, by John Gottman.

The Secrets of Happily Married Men, by Scott Haltzman.

The Secrets of Happily Married Women, by Scott Haltzman.

Rich Dad, Poor Dad, by Robert T. Kiyosaki.

Prayer and Temperament, by Chester Michael and Marie Norrisey.

The Earliest Christologies: Trinitarian Orthodoxy Before Nicaea, by James Papandrea.

Pray (Not Just Say) The Lord's Prayer, by James Papandrea.

The Lessons of St. Francis, by John Michael Talbot.

FILMS EVERYONE SHOULD SEE:

Brother Sun, Sister Moon: A classic 1970s interpretation of the life of Saint Francis.

Bruce Almighty: A film about grace and second chances and about being what you hope to find.

Groundhog Day: A film about living and appreciating life one day at a time.

The Robe: Historical fiction about the earliest Christians; more fiction than history, but still fun.

MUSIC TO ENHANCE PRAYER AND CONTEMPLATION:

Hold Me Lord, by Matthew Baute.

River of Grace, by Matthew Baute www.SongsForPrayer.com.

Psalms, by Joe Hand www.JoeHand.com.

Holy Smoke: The Best of Remember Rome, by Remember Rome www.cdbaby.com/all/remrome.

Hiding Place, by John Michael Talbot.

Simple Heart, by John Michael Talbot www.TroubadourForTheLord.com.

SPIRITUAL RETREATS:

Lessons of St. Francis Retreat at Little Portion Retreat Center.

Come to the Quiet: Christian Meditation at Little Portion Retreat Center www.littleportion.org/retreat-schedule.html.

Check with your church to see if there are any local retreats offered such as Cursillo, Emmaus, Christ Renews His Parish, or Marriage Encounter.

If your marriage is in trouble, consider the Retrouvaille retreat: www.retrouvaille.org.

FOR MORE INFORMATION ON THE AUTHOR, JAMES PAPANDREA:

www.JimPapandrea.com.